MW01622894

THE WRIGHT ADDRESS BOOK

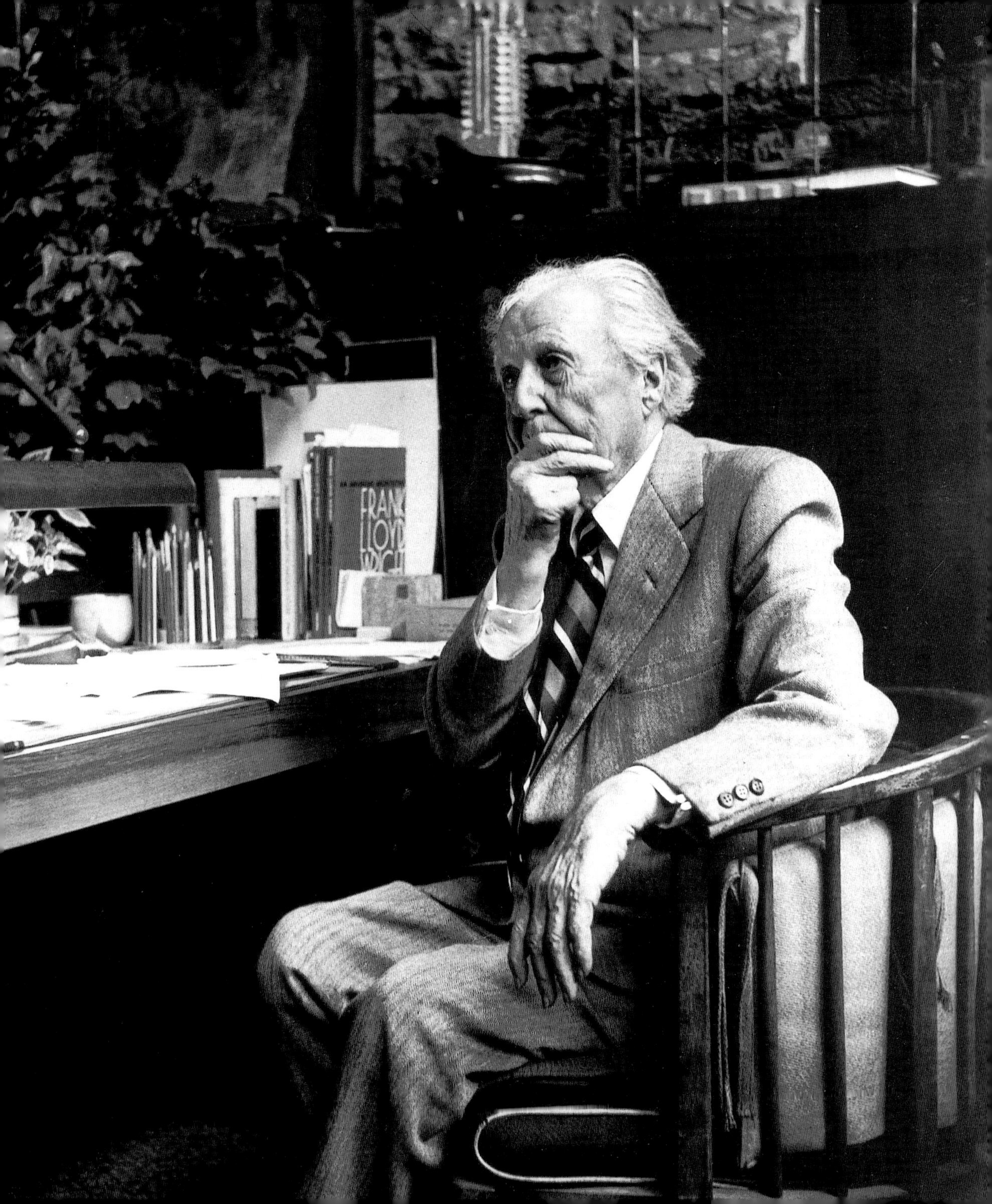

THE WRIGHT ADDRESS BOOK

The Art and Architecture of Frank Lloyd Wright

Domino's Center for Architecture & Design

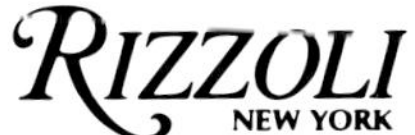

Front cover illustration:

Clerestory window
Avery Coonley Playhouse
Riverside, Illinois, c.1912, (86.25.22)

Frontispiece:
Frank Lloyd Wright (1867-1959)

First Published in the United States of America in 1991
by RIZZOLI INTERNATIONAL PUBLICATIONS, INC.
300 Park Avenue South
New York, NY 10010 and
Domino's Center for Architecture & Design
44 Frank Lloyd Wright Drive
Ann Arbor, Michigan 48106

Designed by Elizabeth Finger
Domino's Center for Architecture & Design wishes to acknowledge the efforts of David A. Hanks & Associates of New York in the preparation of this publication.
Darwin C. Matthews, Director, Domino's Center for Architecture & Design

ISBN 0-8478-1412-2
91 92 93 94 95 / 10 9 8 7 6 5 4 3 2 1
Printed and bound in Hong Kong

Frank Lloyd Wright and Architectural Photography

Throughout his life, photography was an important part of Frank Lloyd Wright's architectural career. In the 1890s, Wright's experiments with this medium included photographs of his family, poetic studies of wild flowers, and views of his home and studio in Oak Park, Illinois. By the 1900s, Wright enlisted the aid of professional photographers to promote his architecture in international periodicals.

The Chicago firm of Henry Fuermann & Sons collaborated with Wright in documenting his early commissions. Evidence indicates that Wright participated in the process by arranging furnishings and selecting perspective views. Their numerous photographs of landscape, exterior architecture, and interiors captured the totality of each Wright commission in a two-dimensional medium. Later in the century, as commissions were demolished or altered, photographs provided a vital record of Wright's lost work.

In 1989, the Domino's Center for Architecture & Design purchased an important collection of 200 glass negatives by Henry Fuermann & Sons, and a few unidentified photographers. This handsome address book features a selection of prints from those negatives, complemented by Wright's decorative designs from the Domino's Collection.

NAME TELEPHONE

ADDRESS

NAME TELEPHONE

ADDRESS

NAME TELEPHONE

ADDRESS

NAME TELEPHONE

ADDRESS

NAME TELEPHONE

ADDRESS

NAME TELEPHONE

ADDRESS

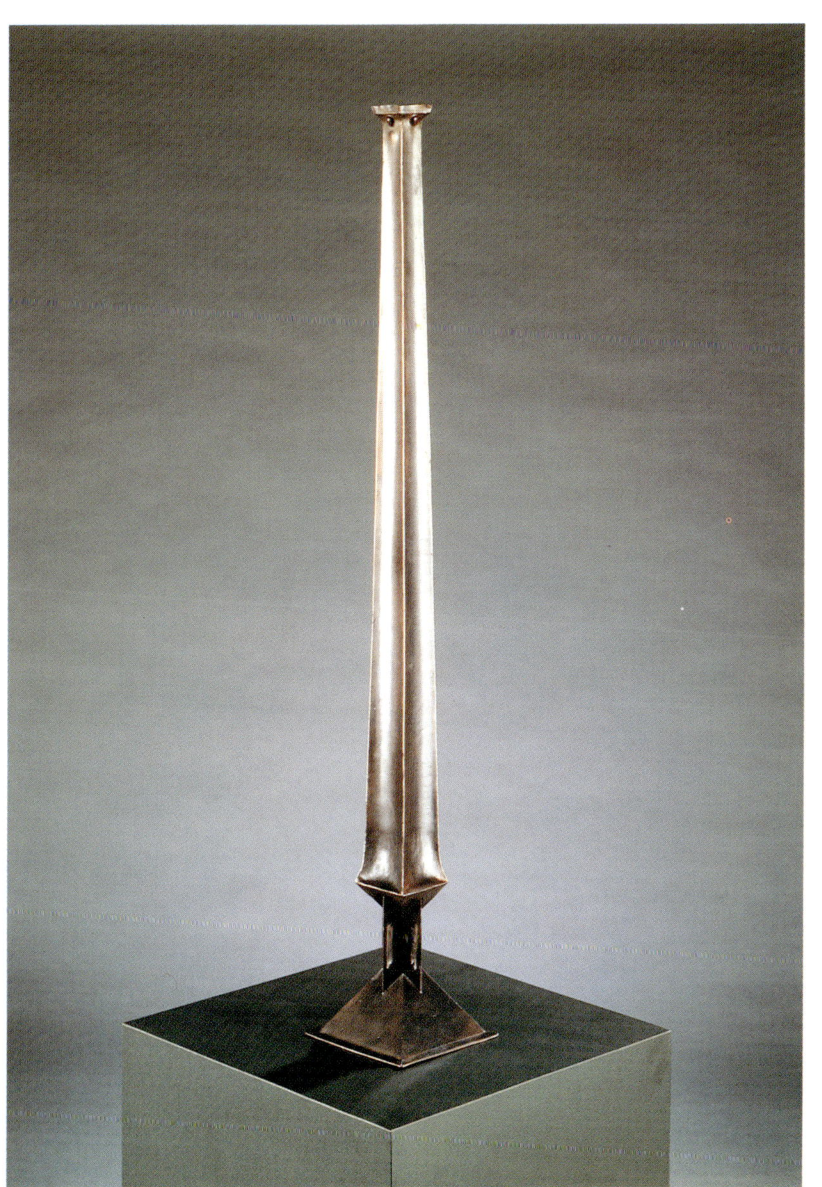

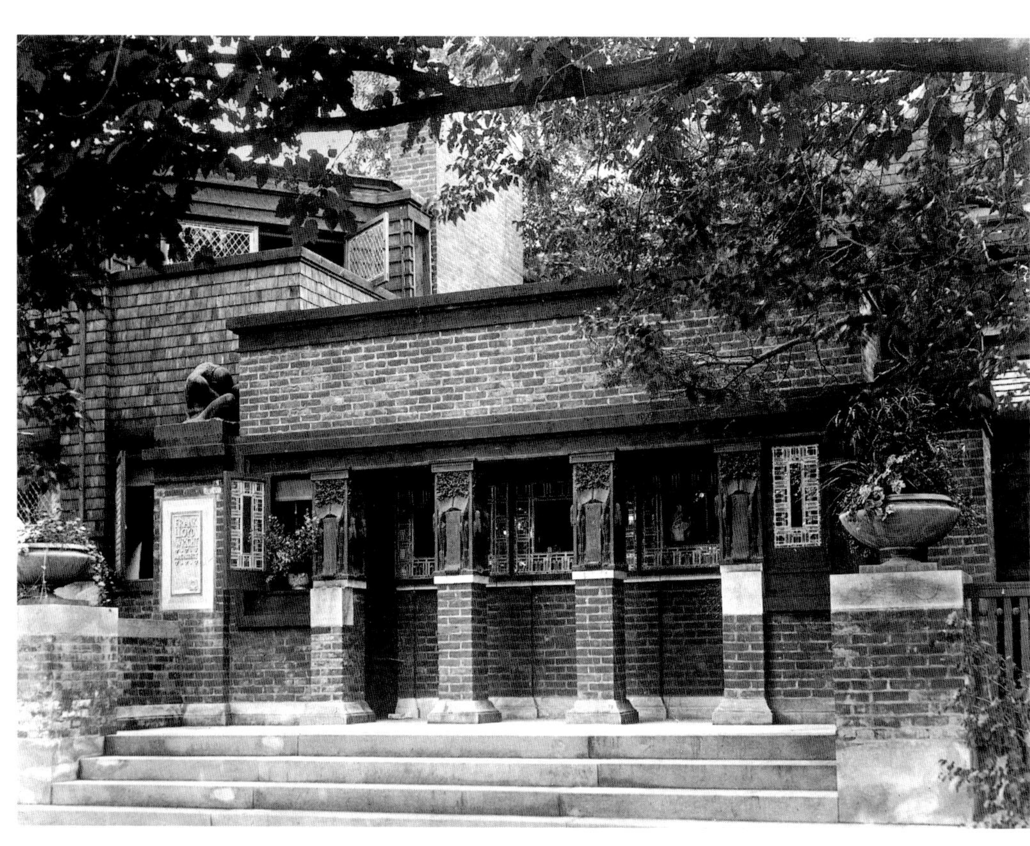

A

NAME TELEPHONE

ADDRESS

NAME TELEPHONE

ADDRESS

NAME TELEPHONE

ADDRESS

NAME TELEPHONE

ADDRESS

NAME TELEPHONE

ADDRESS

NAME TELEPHONE

ADDRESS

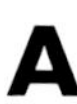

NAME TELEPHONE

ADDRESS

NAME TELEPHONE

ADDRESS

NAME TELEPHONE

ADDRESS

NAME TELEPHONE

ADDRESS

NAME TELEPHONE

ADDRESS

NAME TELEPHONE

ADDRESS

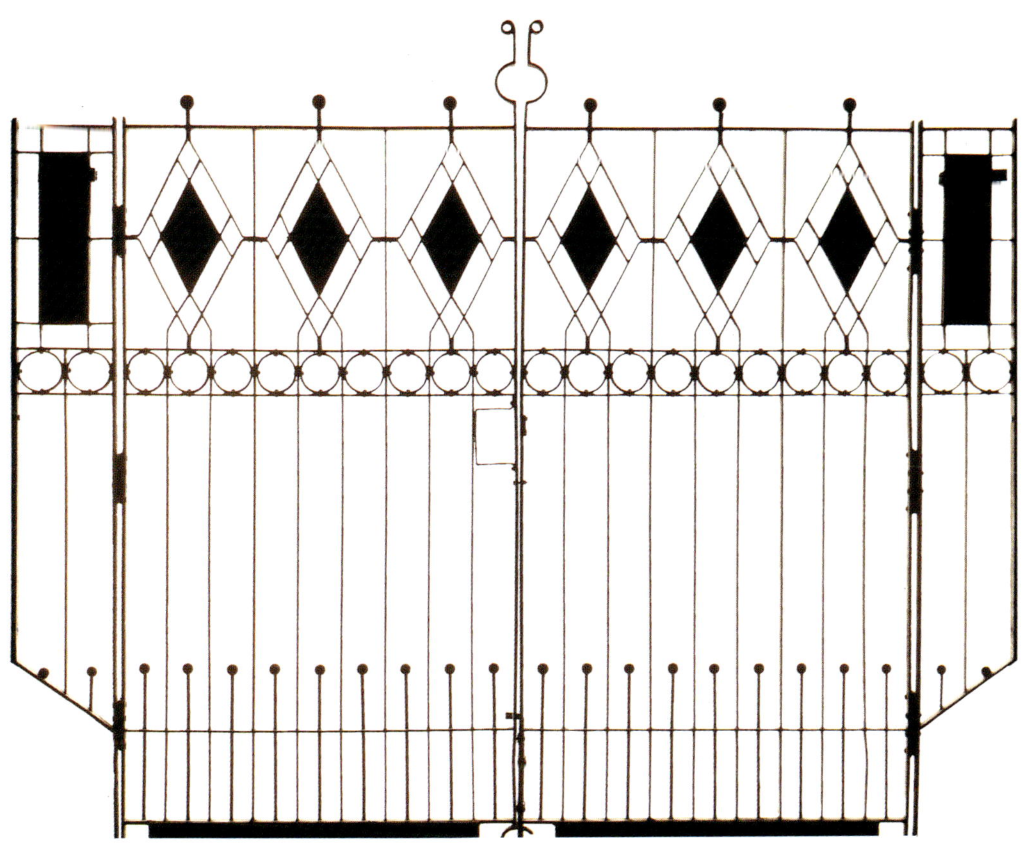

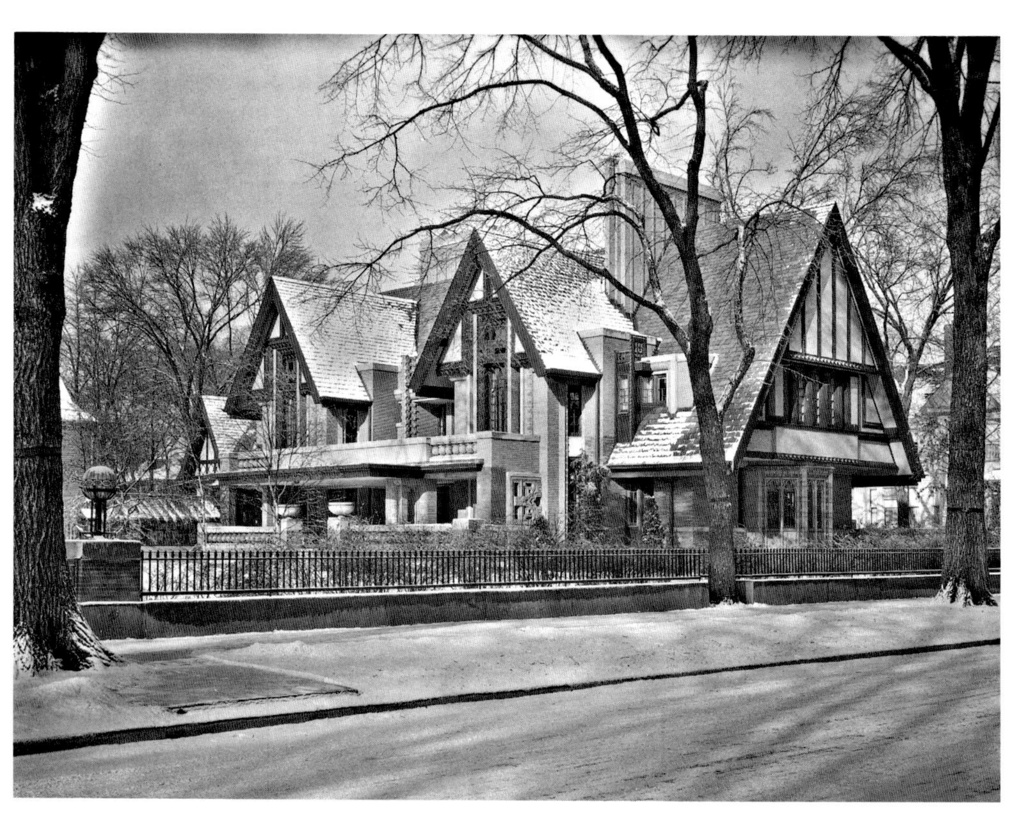

NAME TELEPHONE

ADDRESS

NAME TELEPHONE

ADDRESS

NAME TELEPHONE

ADDRESS

NAME TELEPHONE

ADDRESS

NAME TELEPHONE

ADDRESS

NAME TELEPHONE

ADDRESS

B

NAME TELEPHONE

ADDRESS

NAME TELEPHONE

ADDRESS

NAME TELEPHONE

ADDRESS

NAME TELEPHONE

ADDRESS

NAME TELEPHONE

ADDRESS

NAME TELEPHONE

ADDRESS

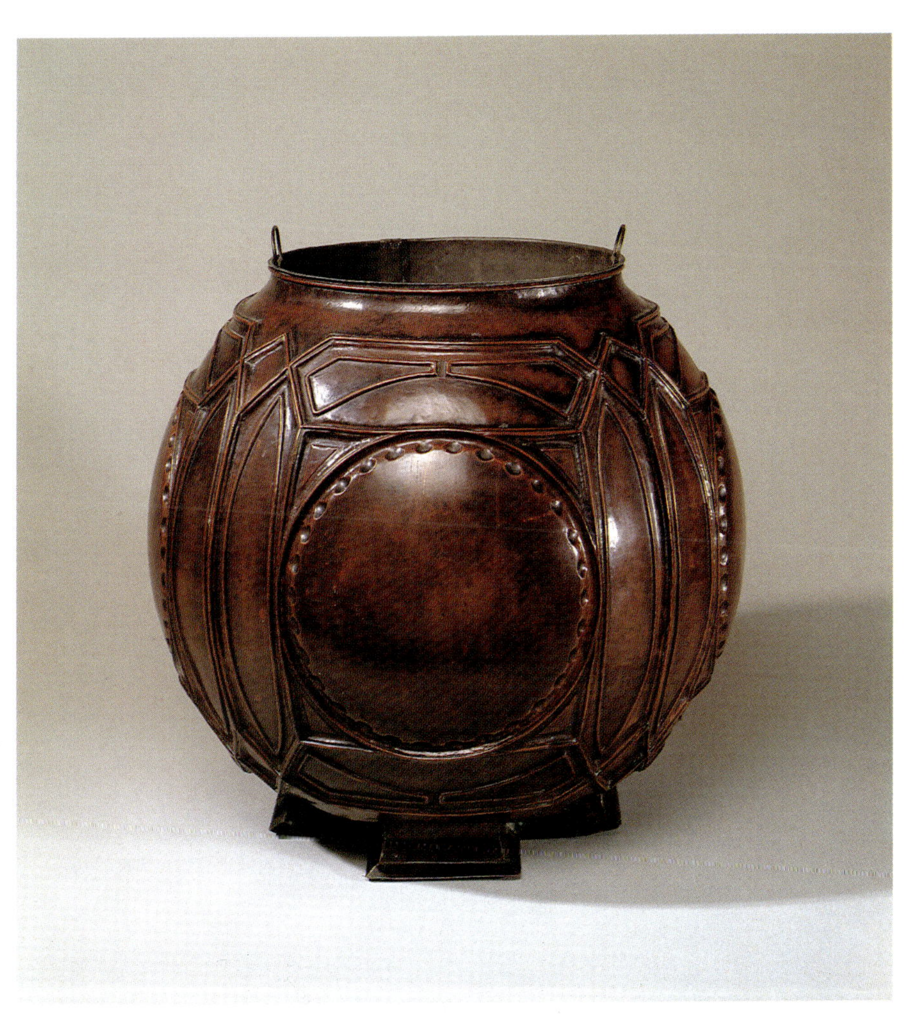

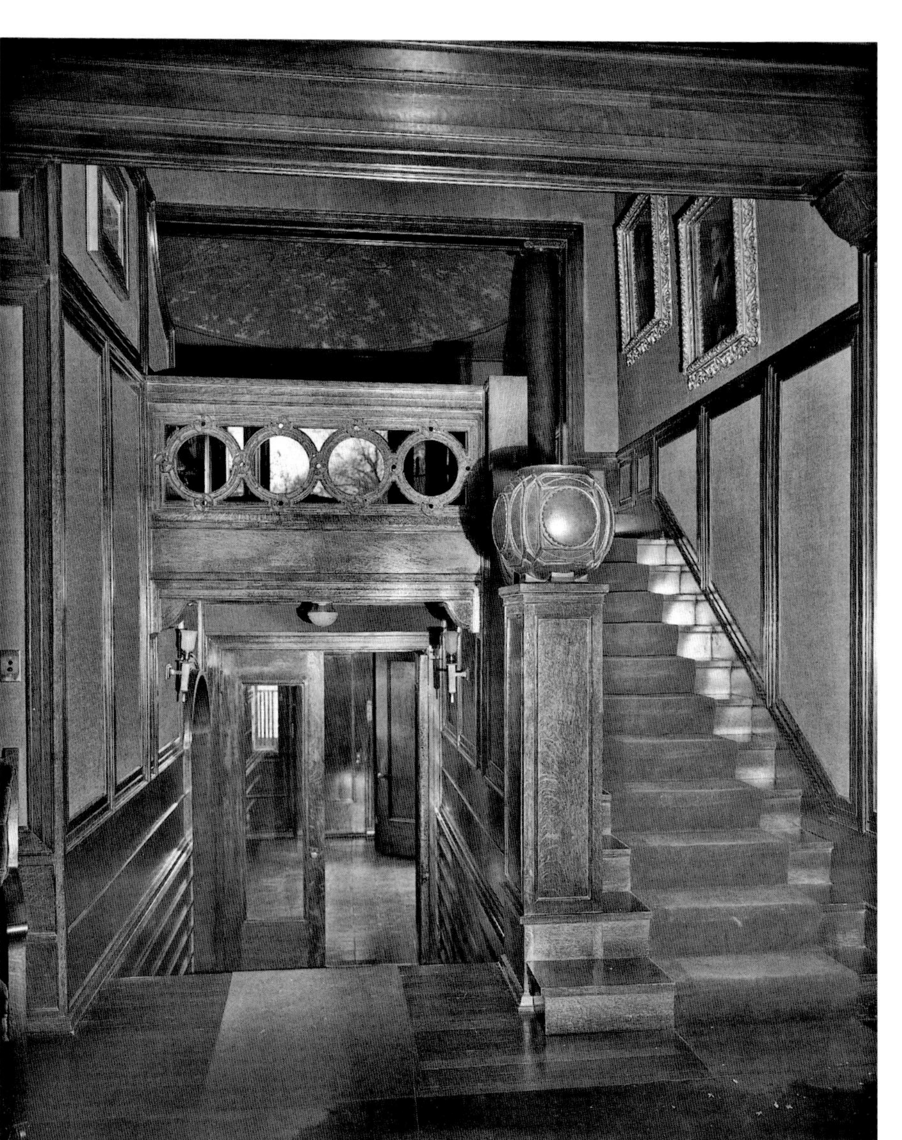

B

NAME TELEPHONE

ADDRESS

NAME TELEPHONE

ADDRESS

NAME TELEPHONE

ADDRESS

NAME TELEPHONE

ADDRESS

NAME TELEPHONE

ADDRESS

NAME TELEPHONE

ADDRESS

C

NAME TELEPHONE

ADDRESS

NAME TELEPHONE

ADDRESS

NAME TELEPHONE

ADDRESS

NAME TELEPHONE

ADDRESS

NAME TELEPHONE

ADDRESS

NAME TELEPHONE

ADDRESS

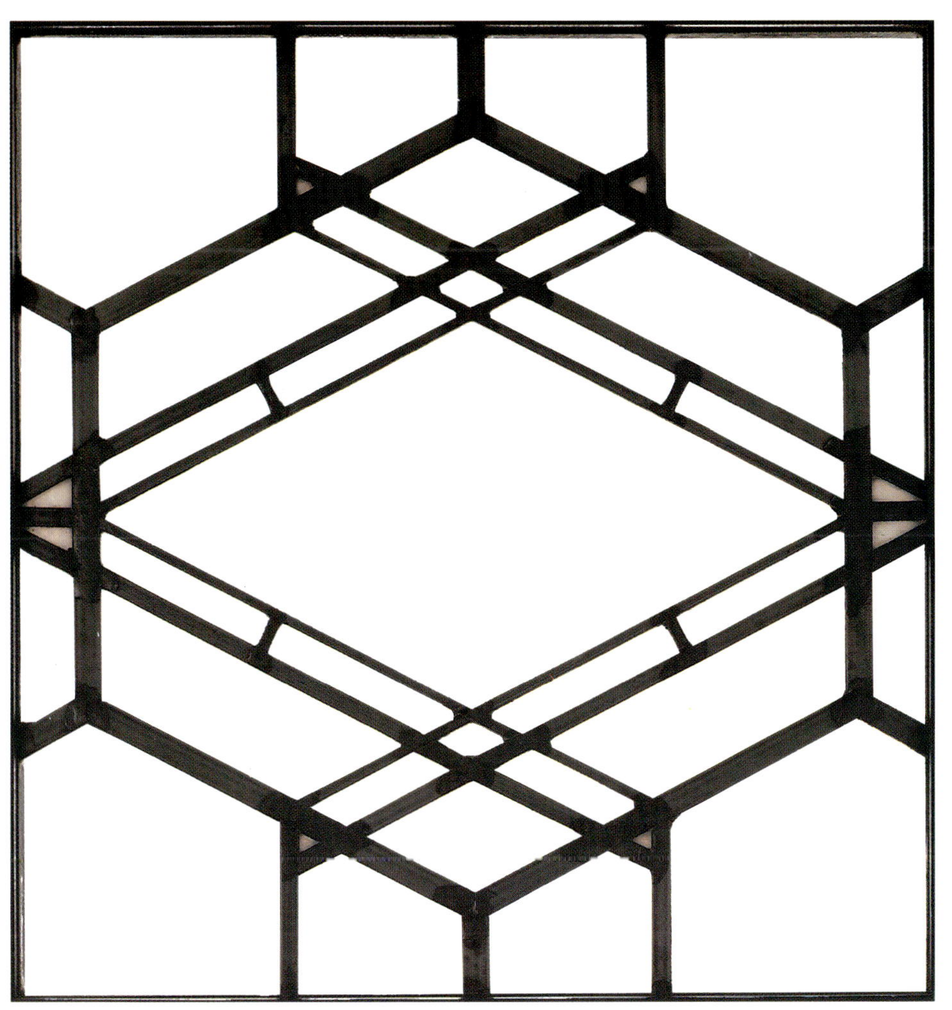

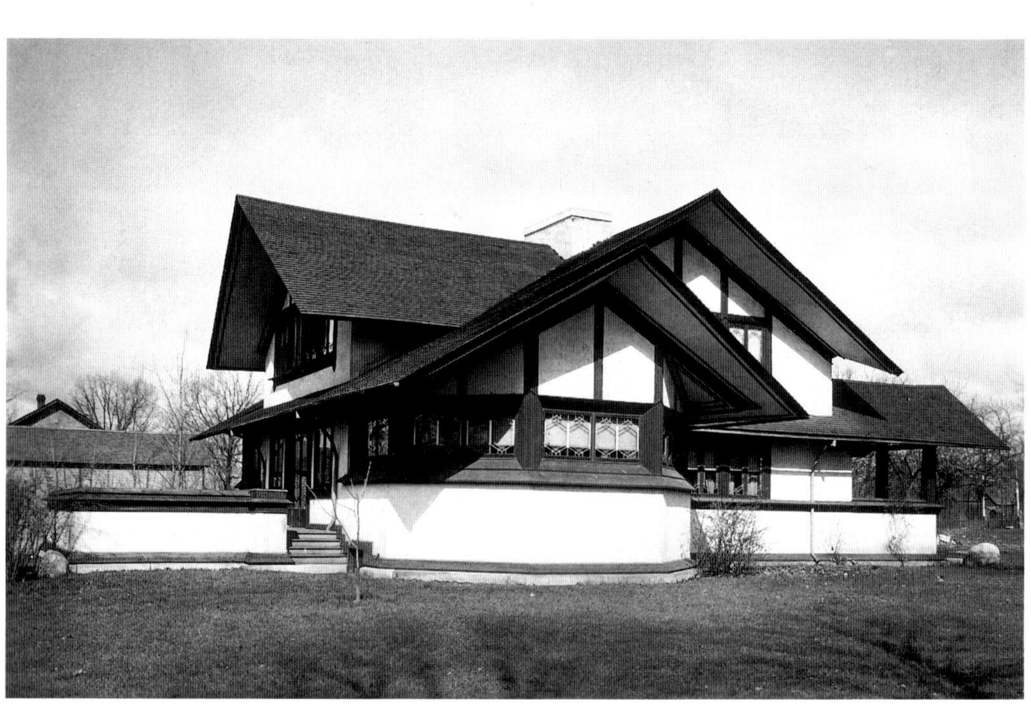

C

NAME TELEPHONE

ADDRESS

NAME TELEPHONE

ADDRESS

NAME TELEPHONE

ADDRESS

NAME TELEPHONE

ADDRESS

NAME TELEPHONE

ADDRESS

NAME TELEPHONE

ADDRESS

C

NAME TELEPHONE

ADDRESS

NAME TELEPHONE

ADDRESS

NAME TELEPHONE

ADDRESS

NAME TELEPHONE

ADDRESS

NAME TELEPHONE

ADDRESS

NAME TELEPHONE

ADDRESS

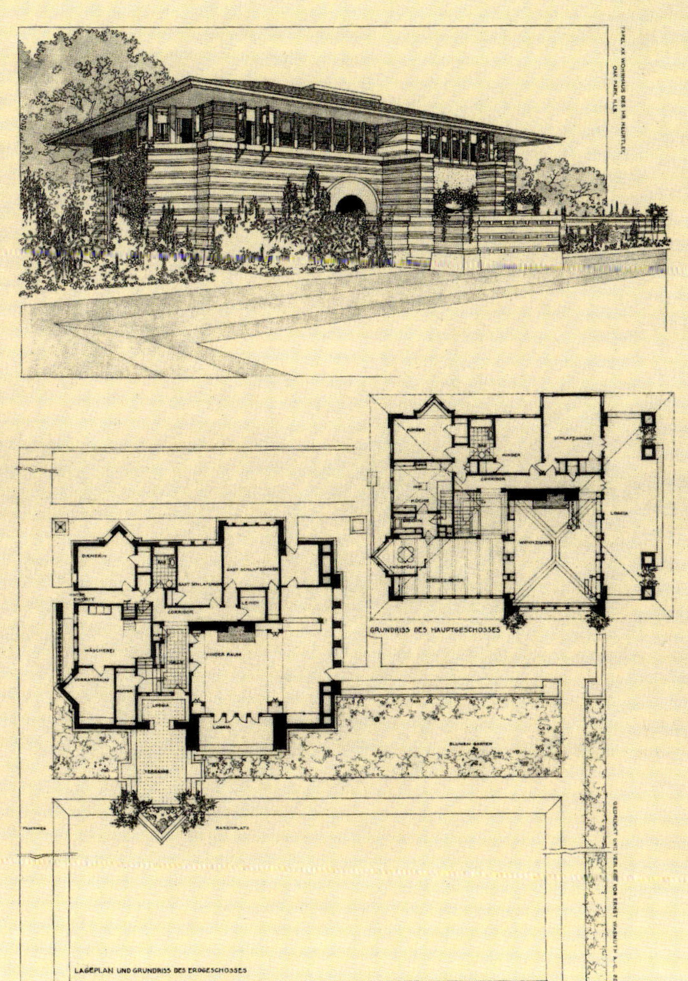
TAFEL XX WOHNHAUS DES HR HEURTLEY,
OAK PARK, ILLS
GRUNDRISS DES HAUPTGESCHOSSES
LAGEPLAN UND GRUNDRISS DES ERDGESCHOSSES
GEDRUCKT UND VERLEGT VON ERNST WASMUTH A.-G. BERLIN

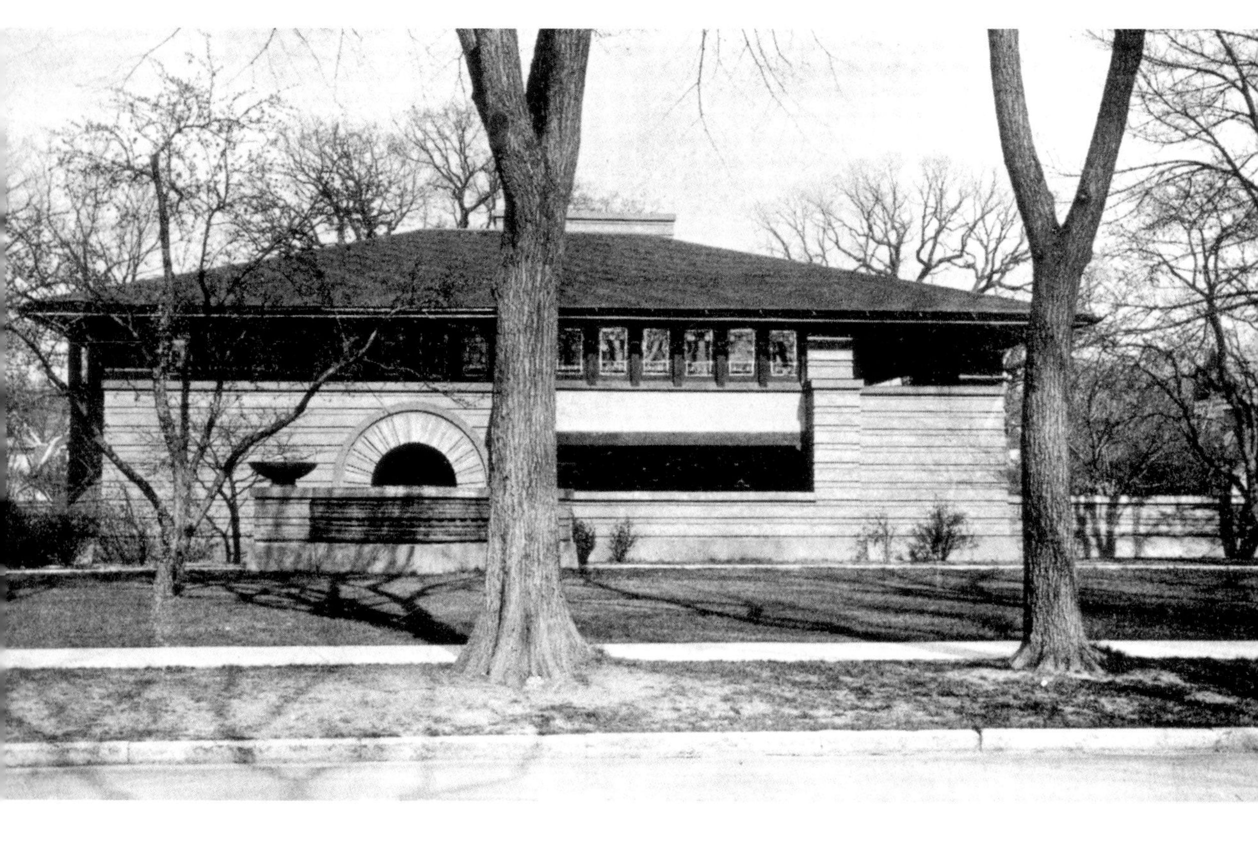

D

NAME TELEPHONE

ADDRESS

NAME TELEPHONE

ADDRESS

NAME TELEPHONE

ADDRESS

NAME TELEPHONE

ADDRESS

NAME TELEPHONE

ADDRESS

NAME TELEPHONE

ADDRESS

D

NAME TELEPHONE

ADDRESS

NAME TELEPHONE

ADDRESS

NAME TELEPHONE

ADDRESS

NAME TELEPHONE

ADDRESS

NAME TELEPHONE

ADDRESS

NAME TELEPHONE

ADDRESS

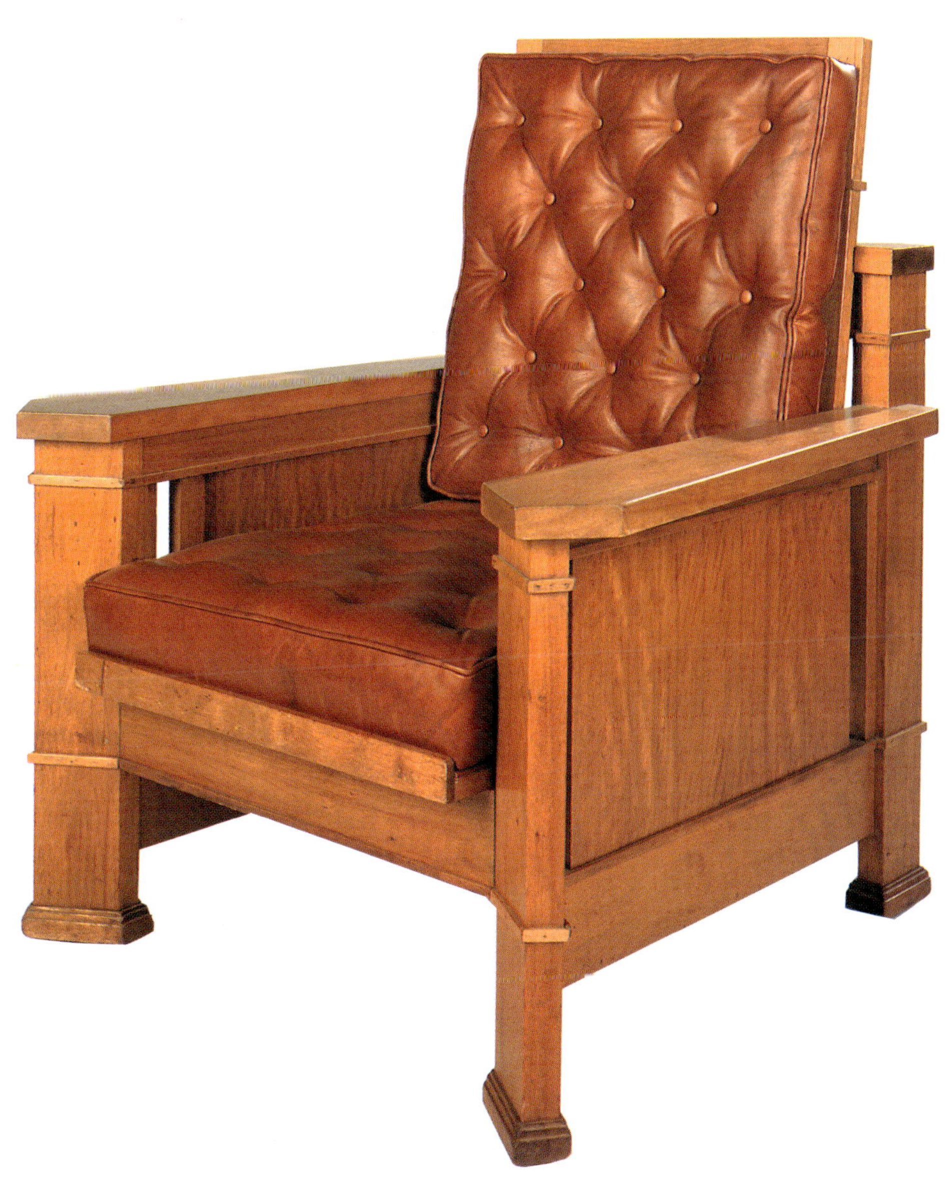

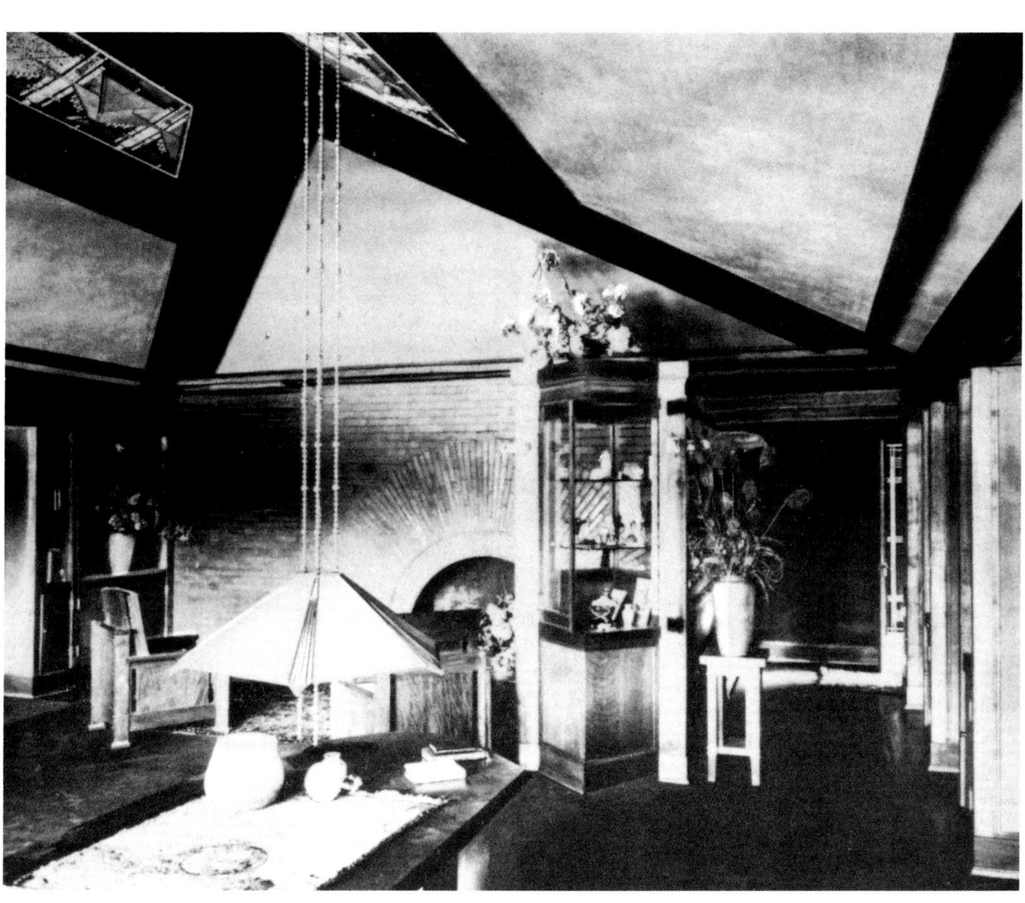

D

NAME TELEPHONE

ADDRESS

NAME TELEPHONE

ADDRESS

NAME TELEPHONE

ADDRESS

NAME TELEPHONE

ADDRESS

NAME TELEPHONE

ADDRESS

NAME TELEPHONE

ADDRESS

EF

NAME TELEPHONE

ADDRESS

NAME TELEPHONE

ADDRESS

NAME TELEPHONE

ADDRESS

NAME TELEPHONE

ADDRESS

NAME TELEPHONE

ADDRESS

NAME TELEPHONE

ADDRESS

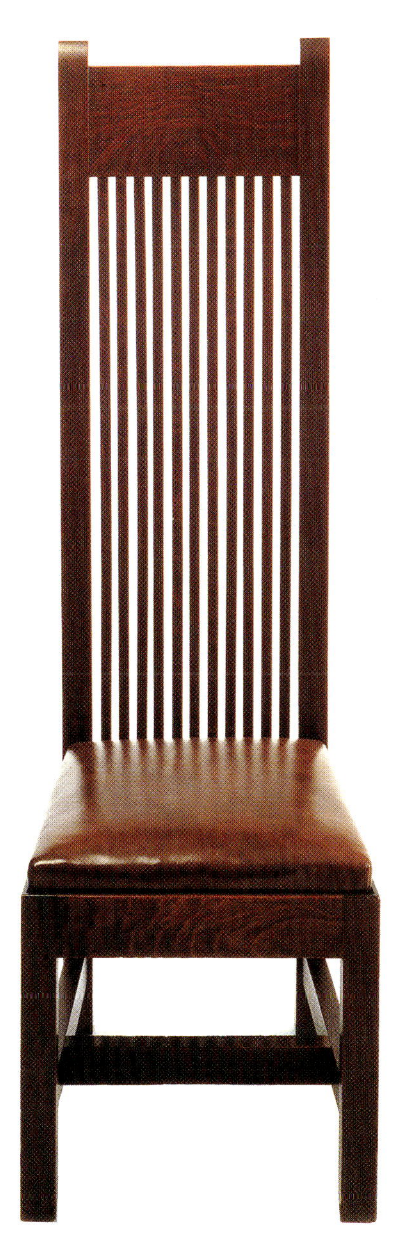

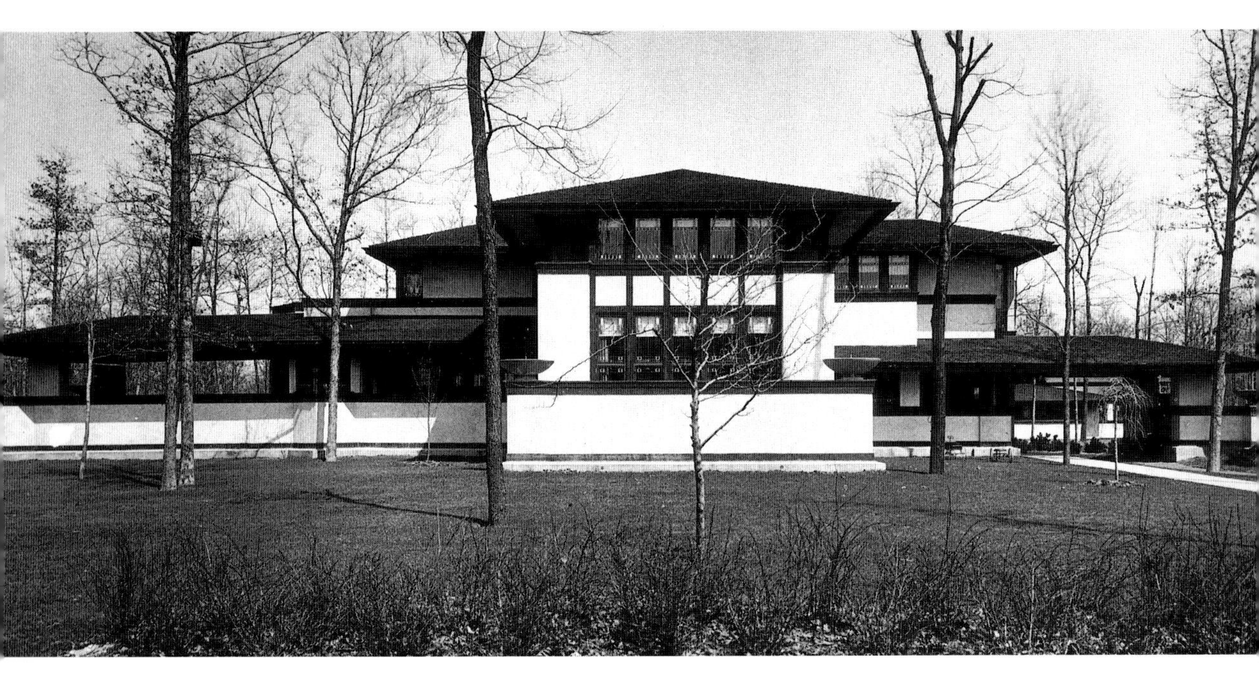

NAME TELEPHONE

ADDRESS

NAME TELEPHONE

ADDRESS

NAME TELEPHONE

ADDRESS

NAME TELEPHONE

ADDRESS

NAME TELEPHONE

ADDRESS

NAME TELEPHONE

ADDRESS

EF

NAME TELEPHONE

ADDRESS

NAME TELEPHONE

ADDRESS

NAME TELEPHONE

ADDRESS

NAME TELEPHONE

ADDRESS

NAME TELEPHONE

ADDRESS

NAME TELEPHONE

ADDRESS

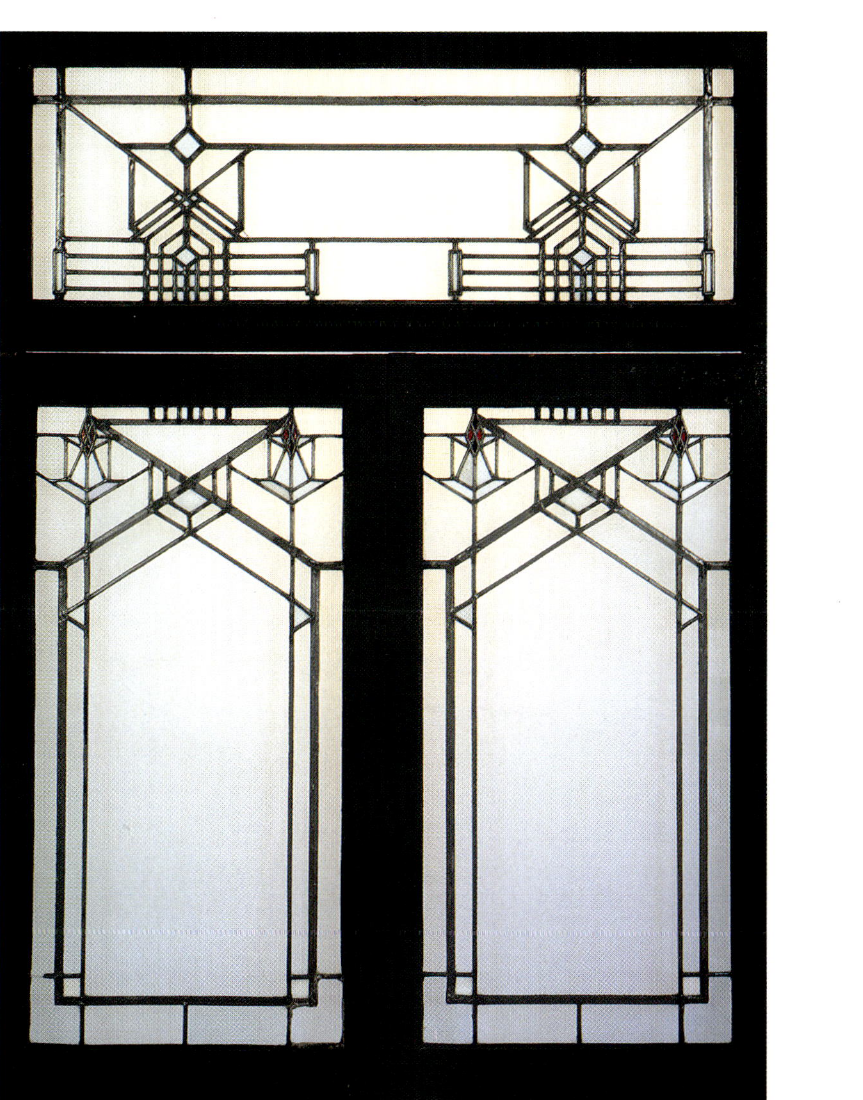

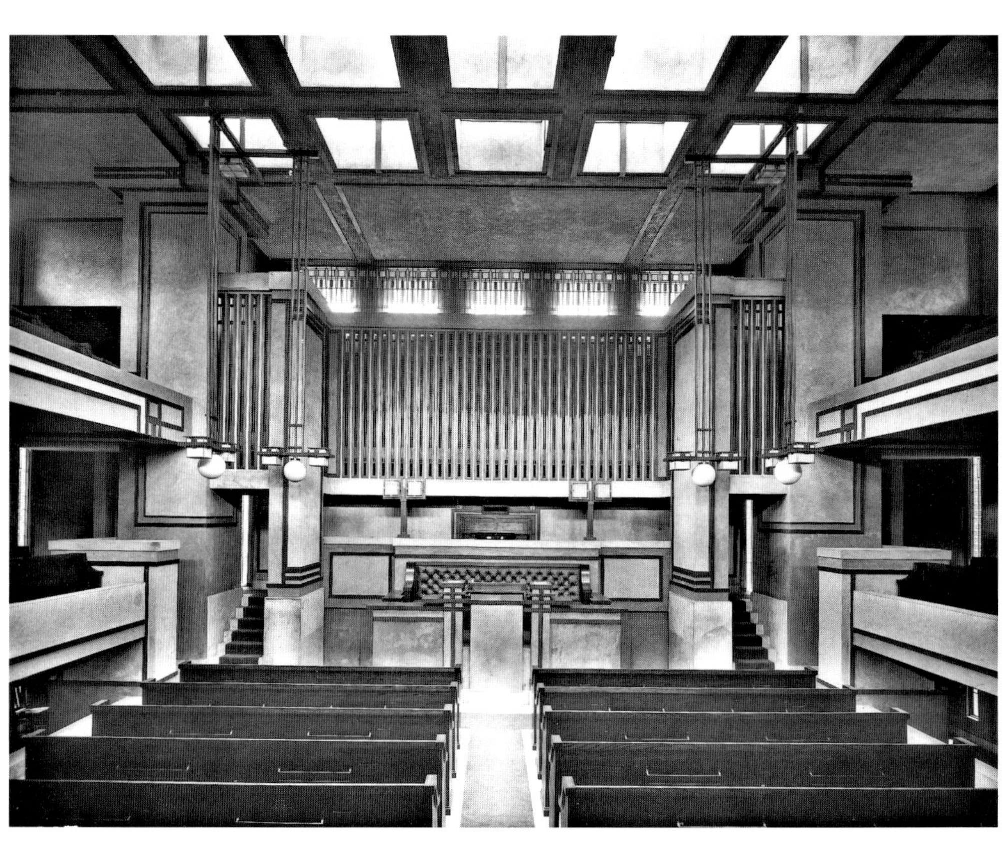

G

NAME TELEPHONE

ADDRESS

NAME TELEPHONE

ADDRESS

NAME TELEPHONE

ADDRESS

NAME TELEPHONE

ADDRESS

NAME TELEPHONE

ADDRESS

NAME TELEPHONE

ADDRESS

G

NAME TELEPHONE

ADDRESS

NAME TELEPHONE

ADDRESS

NAME TELEPHONE

ADDRESS

NAME TELEPHONE

ADDRESS

NAME TELEPHONE

ADDRESS

NAME TELEPHONE

ADDRESS

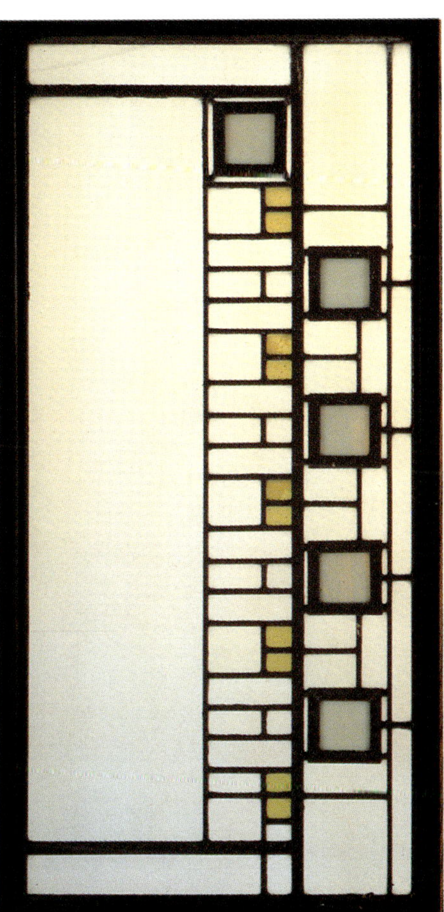
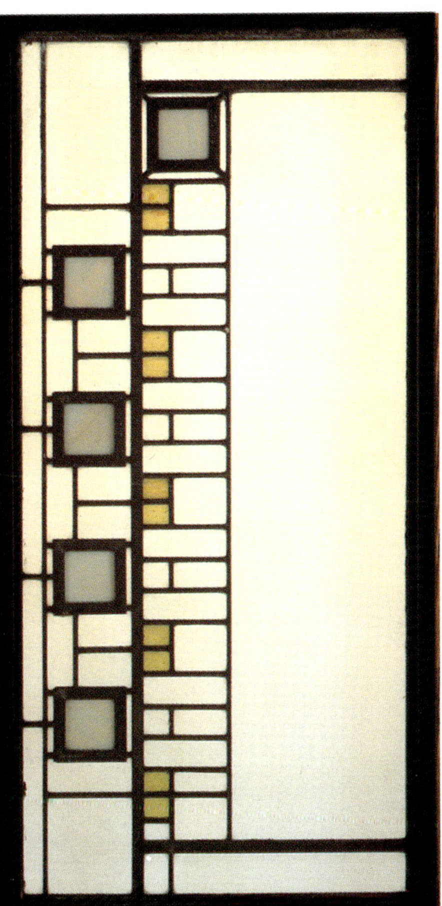

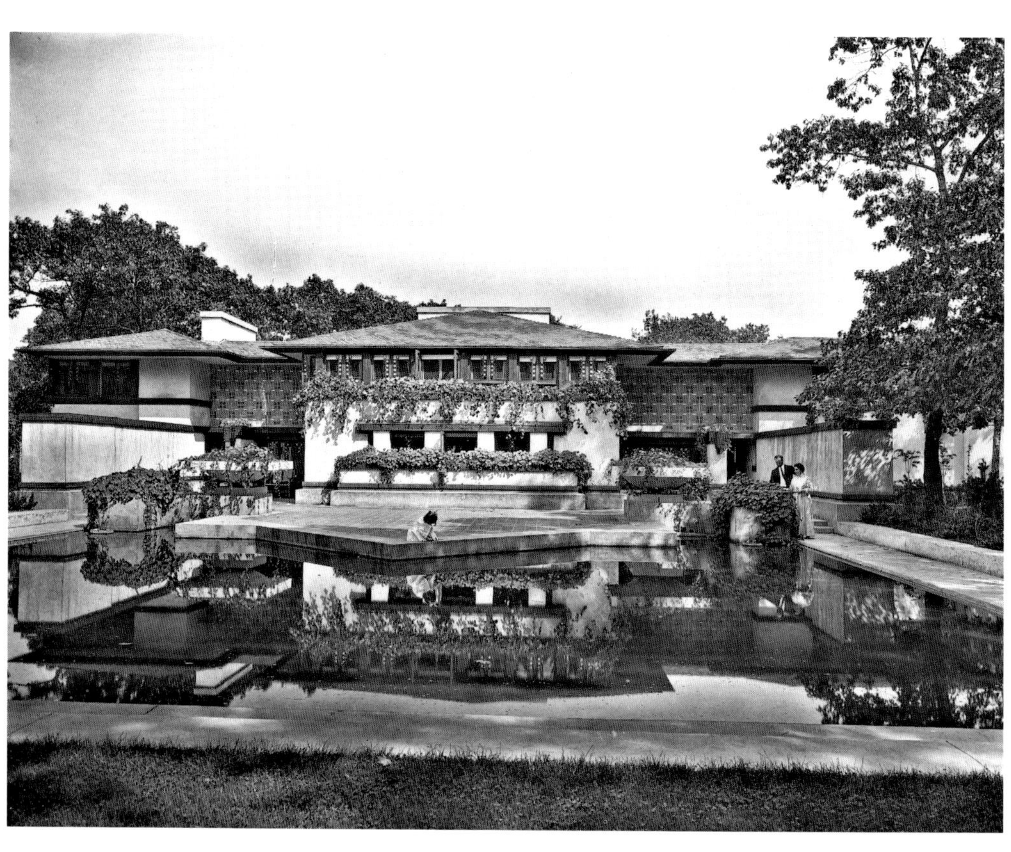

G

NAME TELEPHONE

ADDRESS

NAME TELEPHONE

ADDRESS

NAME TELEPHONE

ADDRESS

NAME TELEPHONE

ADDRESS

NAME TELEPHONE

ADDRESS

NAME TELEPHONE

ADDRESS

H

NAME TELEPHONE

ADDRESS

NAME TELEPHONE

ADDRESS

NAME TELEPHONE

ADDRESS

NAME TELEPHONE

ADDRESS

NAME TELEPHONE

ADDRESS

NAME TELEPHONE

ADDRESS

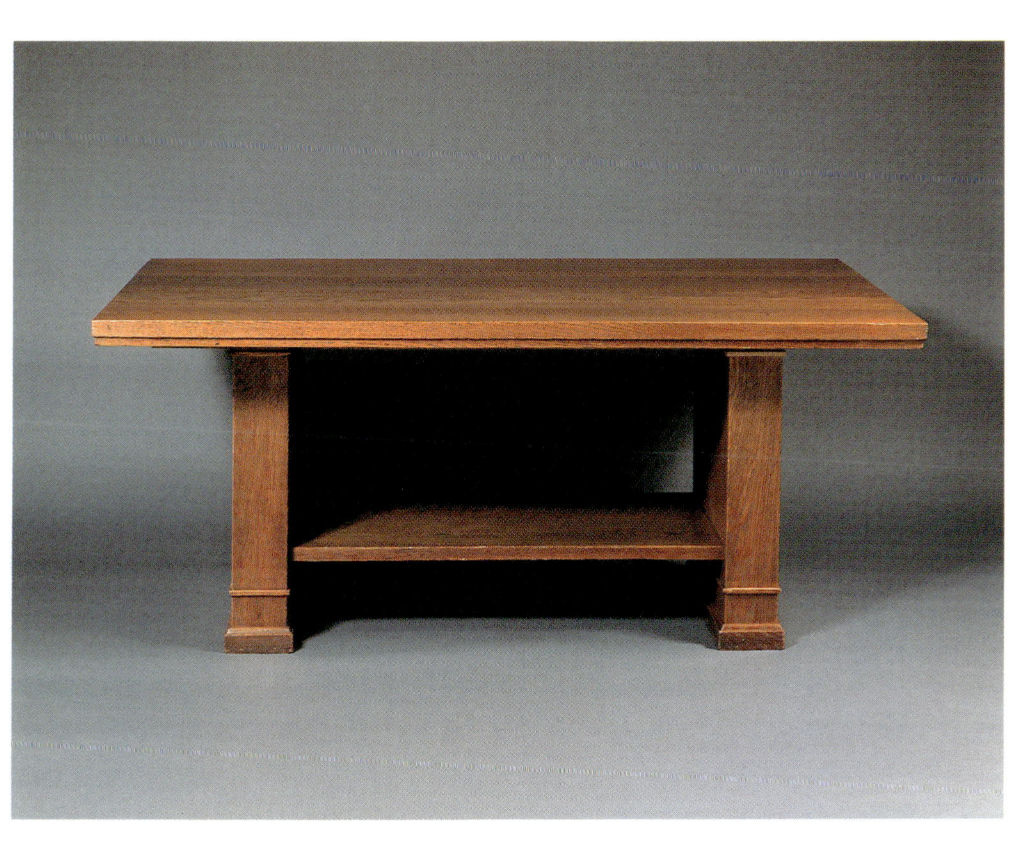

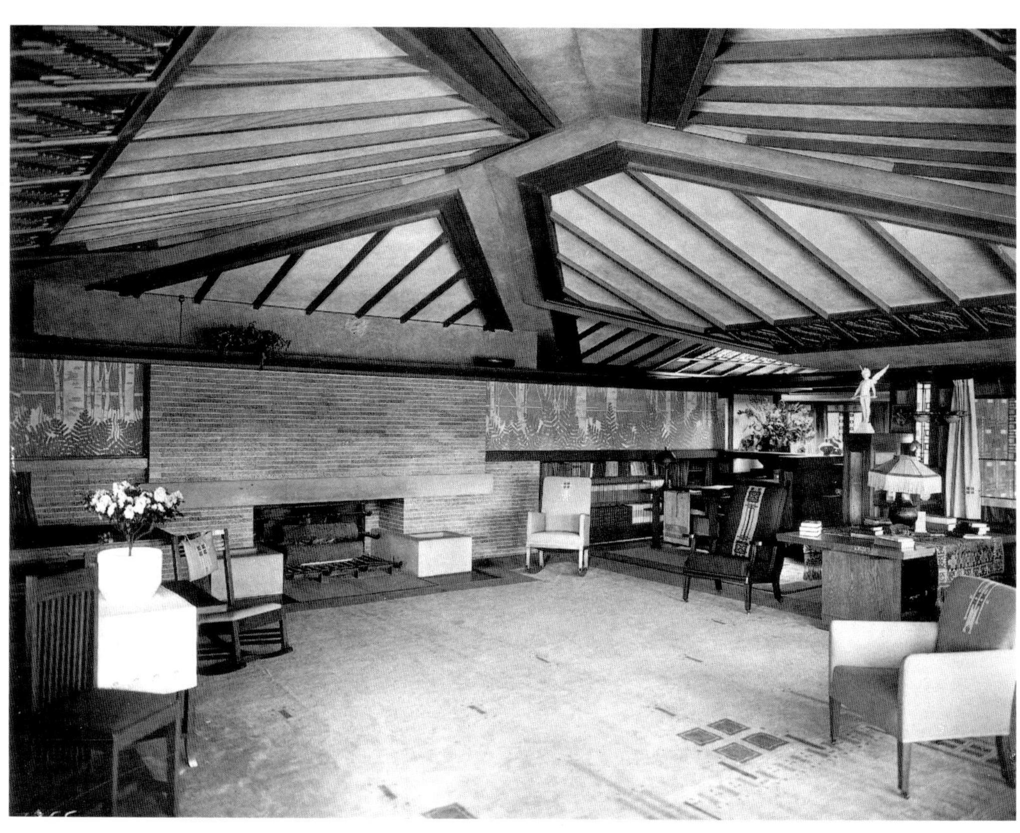

NAME TELEPHONE

ADDRESS

NAME TELEPHONE

ADDRESS

NAME TELEPHONE

ADDRESS

NAME TELEPHONE

ADDRESS

NAME TELEPHONE

ADDRESS

NAME TELEPHONE

ADDRESS

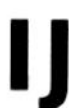

NAME TELEPHONE

ADDRESS

NAME TELEPHONE

ADDRESS

NAME TELEPHONE

ADDRESS

NAME TELEPHONE

ADDRESS

NAME TELEPHONE

ADDRESS

NAME TELEPHONE

ADDRESS

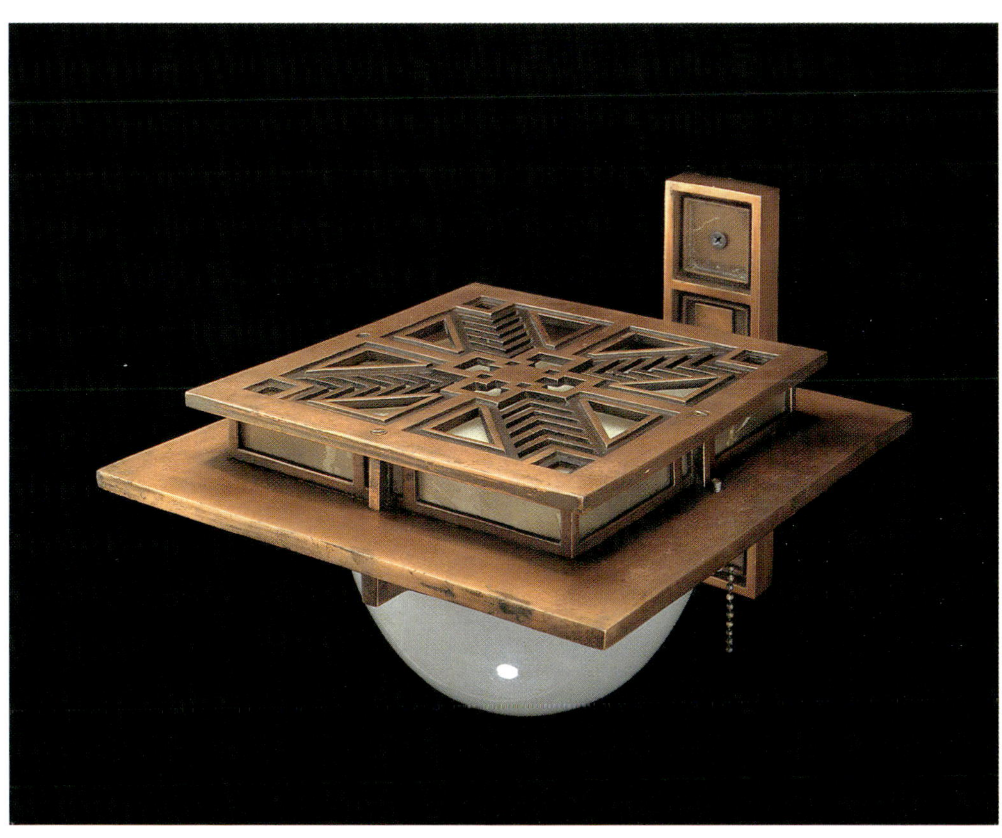

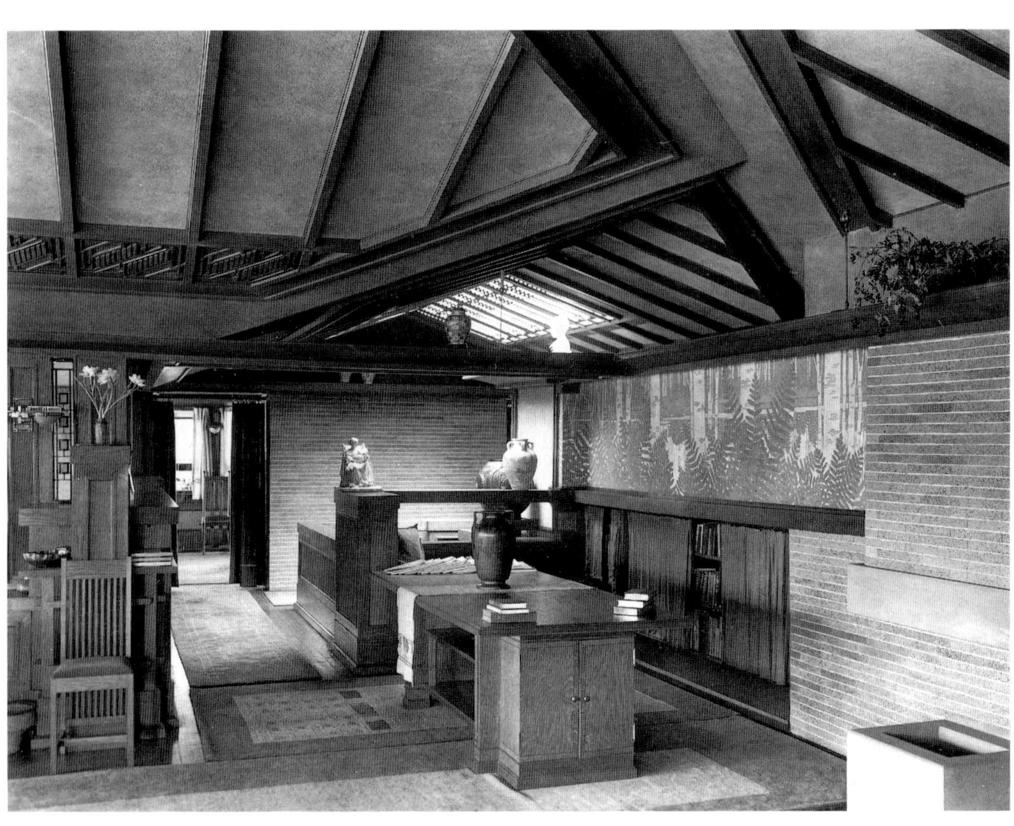

NAME TELEPHONE

ADDRESS

NAME TELEPHONE

ADDRESS

NAME TELEPHONE

ADDRESS

NAME TELEPHONE

ADDRESS

NAME TELEPHONE

ADDRESS

NAME TELEPHONE

ADDRESS

K

NAME TELEPHONE

ADDRESS

NAME TELEPHONE

ADDRESS

NAME TELEPHONE

ADDRESS

NAME TELEPHONE

ADDRESS

NAME TELEPHONE

ADDRESS

NAME TELEPHONE

ADDRESS

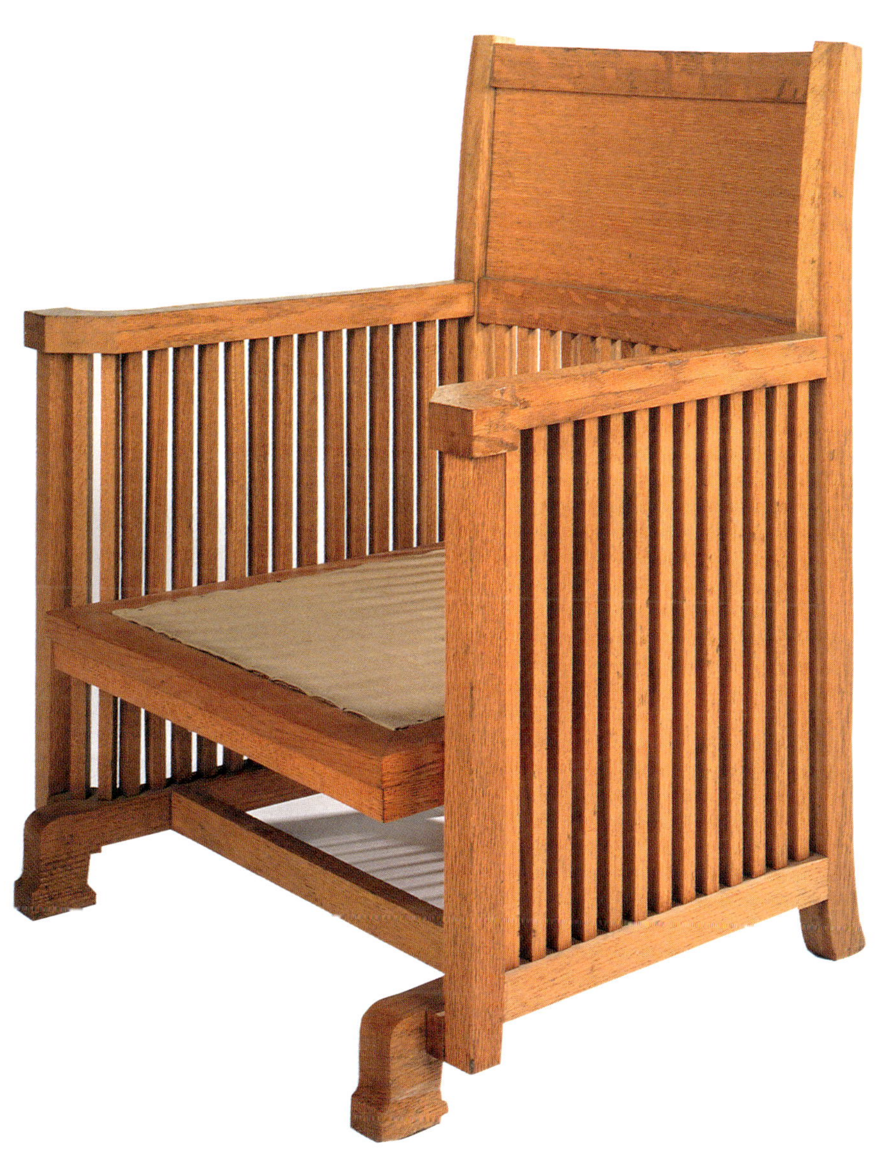

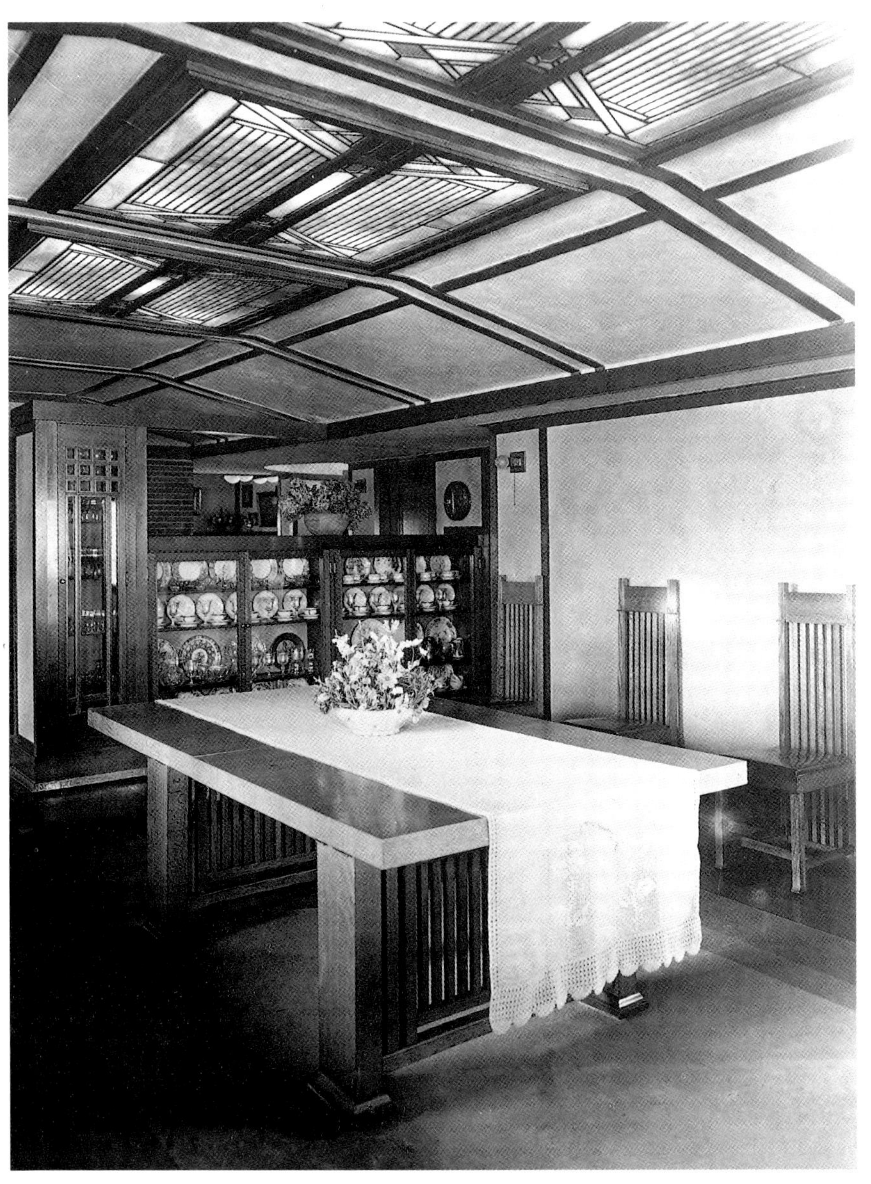

K

NAME TELEPHONE

ADDRESS

NAME TELEPHONE

ADDRESS

NAME TELEPHONE

ADDRESS

NAME TELEPHONE

ADDRESS

NAME TELEPHONE

ADDRESS

NAME TELEPHONE

ADDRESS

L

NAME TELEPHONE

ADDRESS

NAME TELEPHONE

ADDRESS

NAME TELEPHONE

ADDRESS

NAME TELEPHONE

ADDRESS

NAME TELEPHONE

ADDRESS

NAME TELEPHONE

ADDRESS

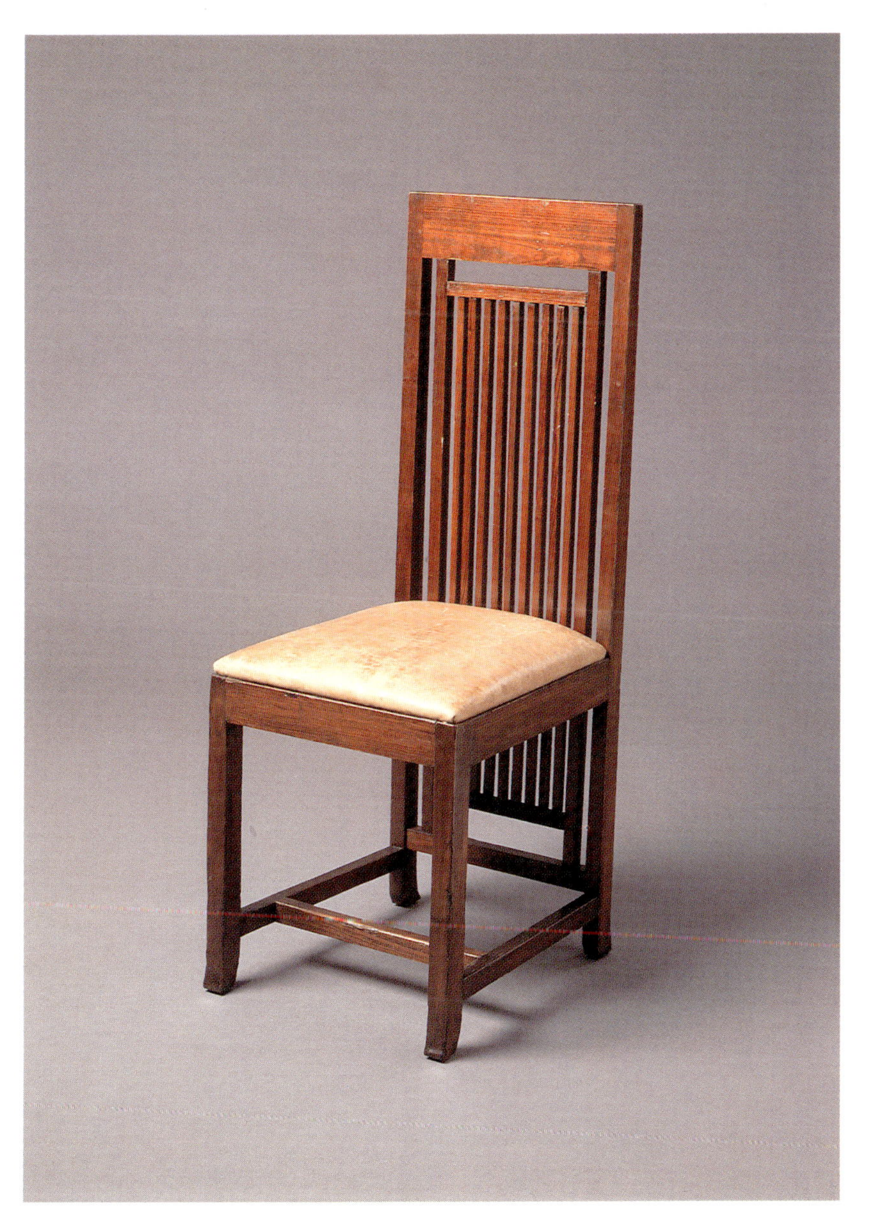

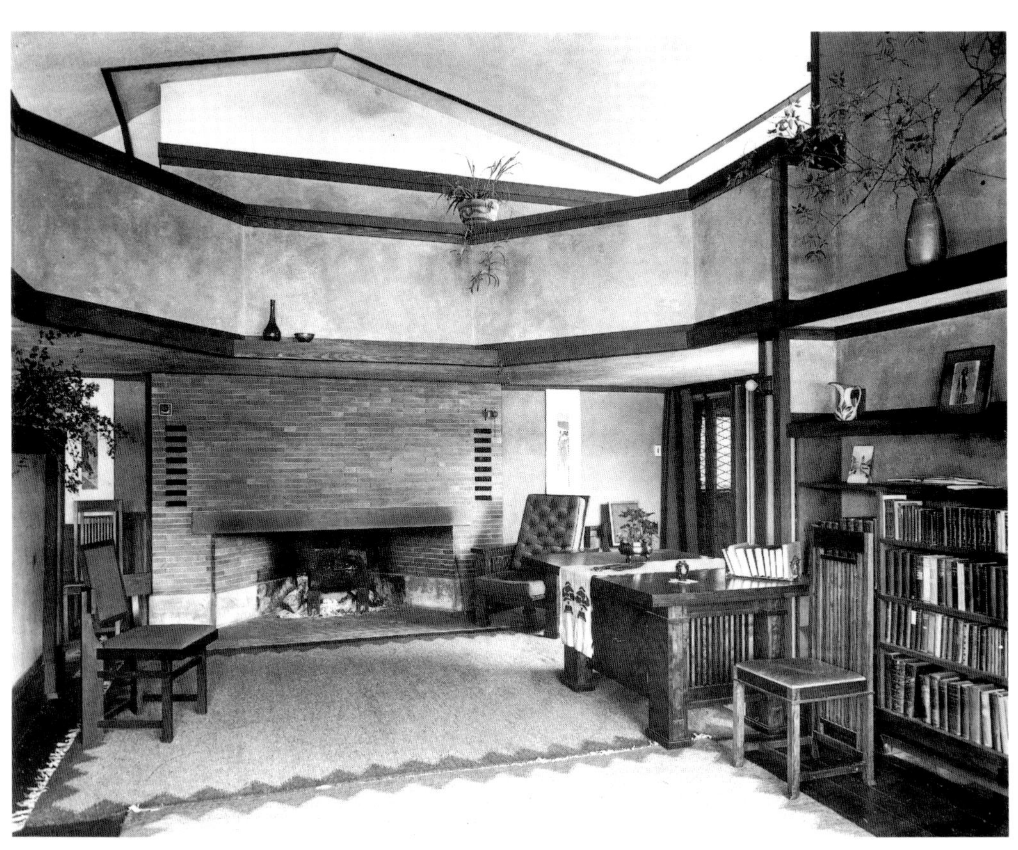

L

NAME TELEPHONE

ADDRESS

NAME TELEPHONE

ADDRESS

NAME TELEPHONE

ADDRESS

NAME TELEPHONE

ADDRESS

NAME TELEPHONE

ADDRESS

NAME TELEPHONE

ADDRESS

L

NAME TELEPHONE

ADDRESS

NAME TELEPHONE

ADDRESS

NAME TELEPHONE

ADDRESS

NAME TELEPHONE

ADDRESS

NAME TELEPHONE

ADDRESS

NAME TELEPHONE

ADDRESS

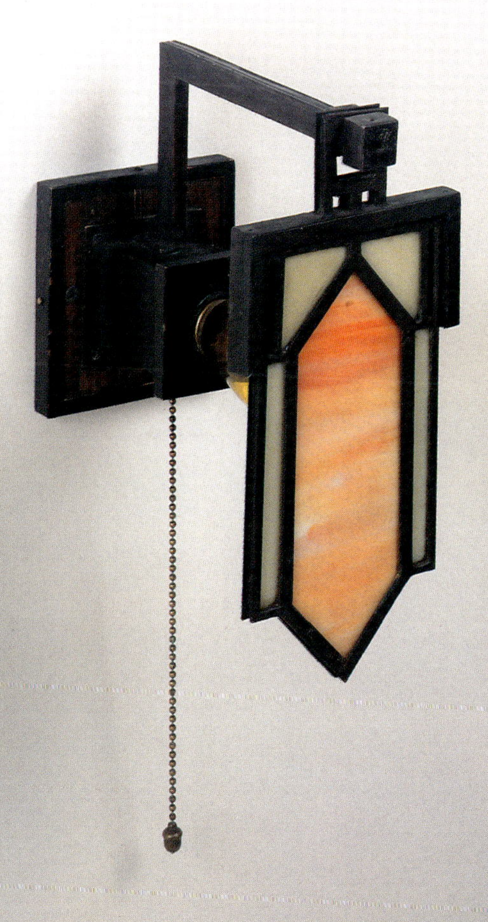

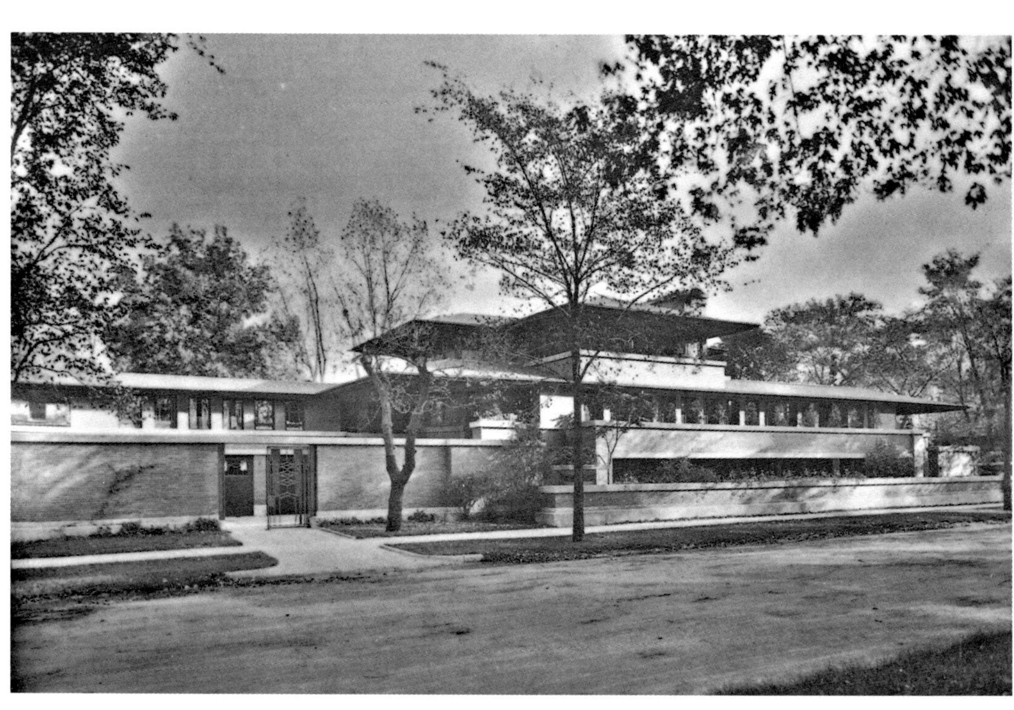

M

NAME TELEPHONE

ADDRESS

NAME TELEPHONE

ADDRESS

NAME TELEPHONE

ADDRESS

NAME TELEPHONE

ADDRESS

NAME TELEPHONE

ADDRESS

NAME TELEPHONE

ADDRESS

NAME TELEPHONE

ADDRESS

NAME TELEPHONE

ADDRESS

NAME TELEPHONE

ADDRESS

NAME TELEPHONE

ADDRESS

NAME TELEPHONE

ADDRESS

NAME TELEPHONE

ADDRESS

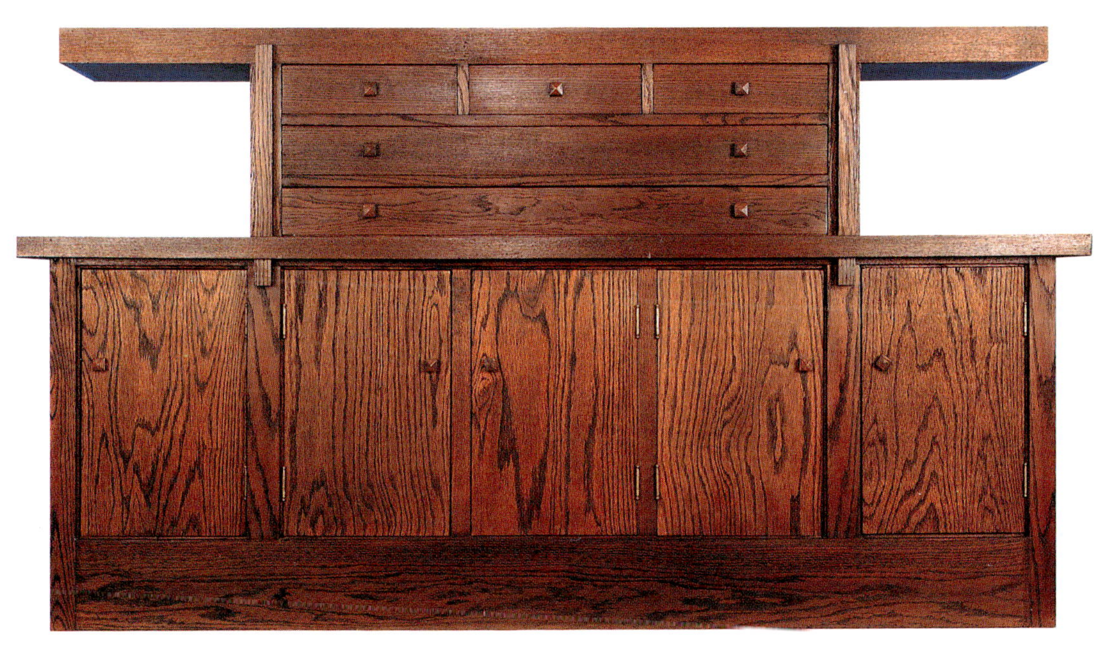

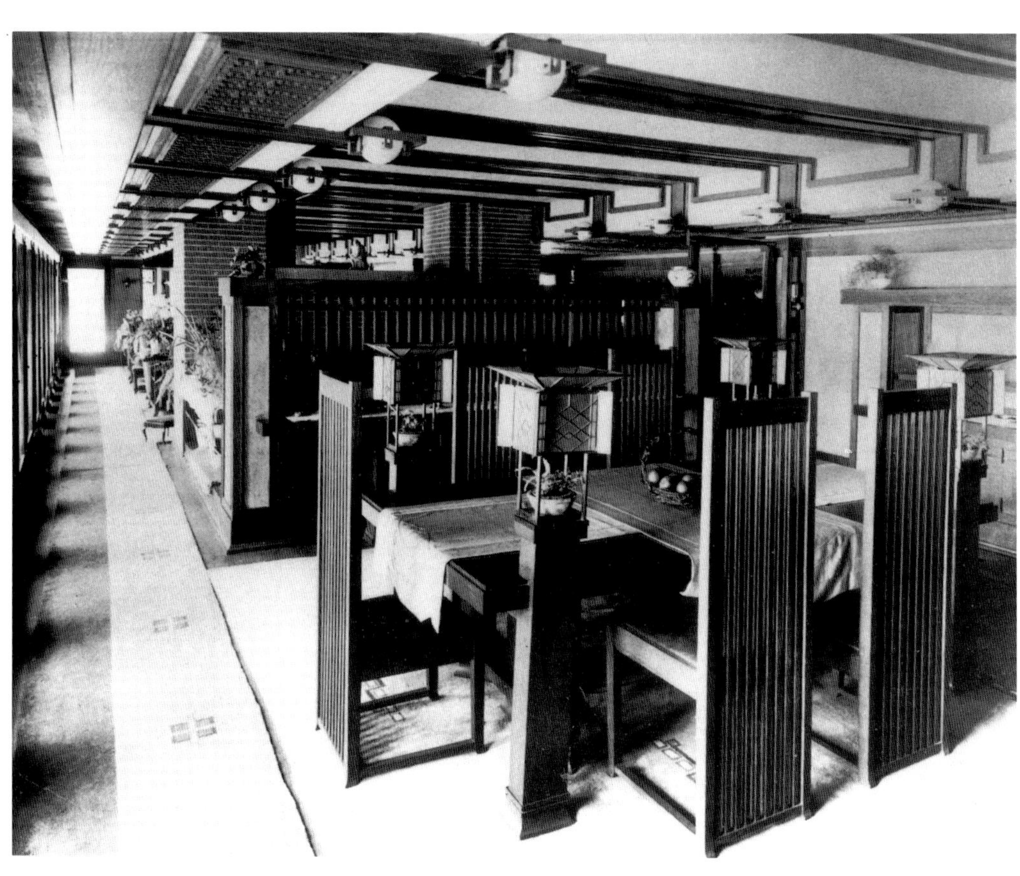

M

NAME TELEPHONE

ADDRESS

NAME TELEPHONE

ADDRESS

NAME TELEPHONE

ADDRESS

NAME TELEPHONE

ADDRESS

NAME TELEPHONE

ADDRESS

NAME TELEPHONE

ADDRESS

N

NAME TELEPHONE

ADDRESS

NAME TELEPHONE

ADDRESS

NAME TELEPHONE

ADDRESS

NAME TELEPHONE

ADDRESS

NAME TELEPHONE

ADDRESS

NAME TELEPHONE

ADDRESS

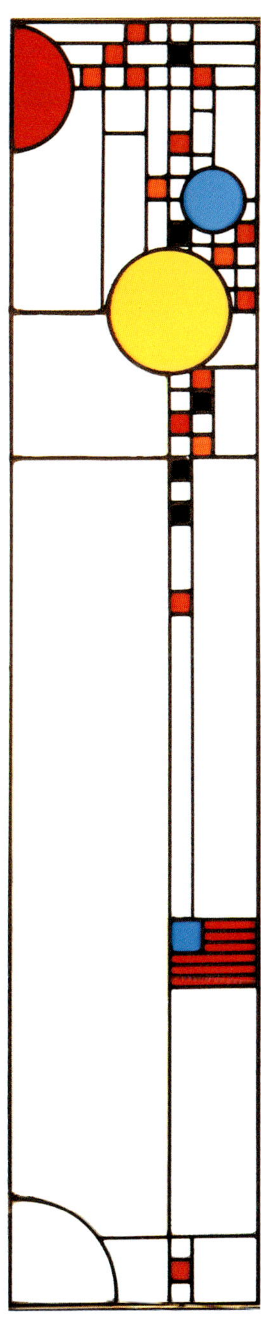

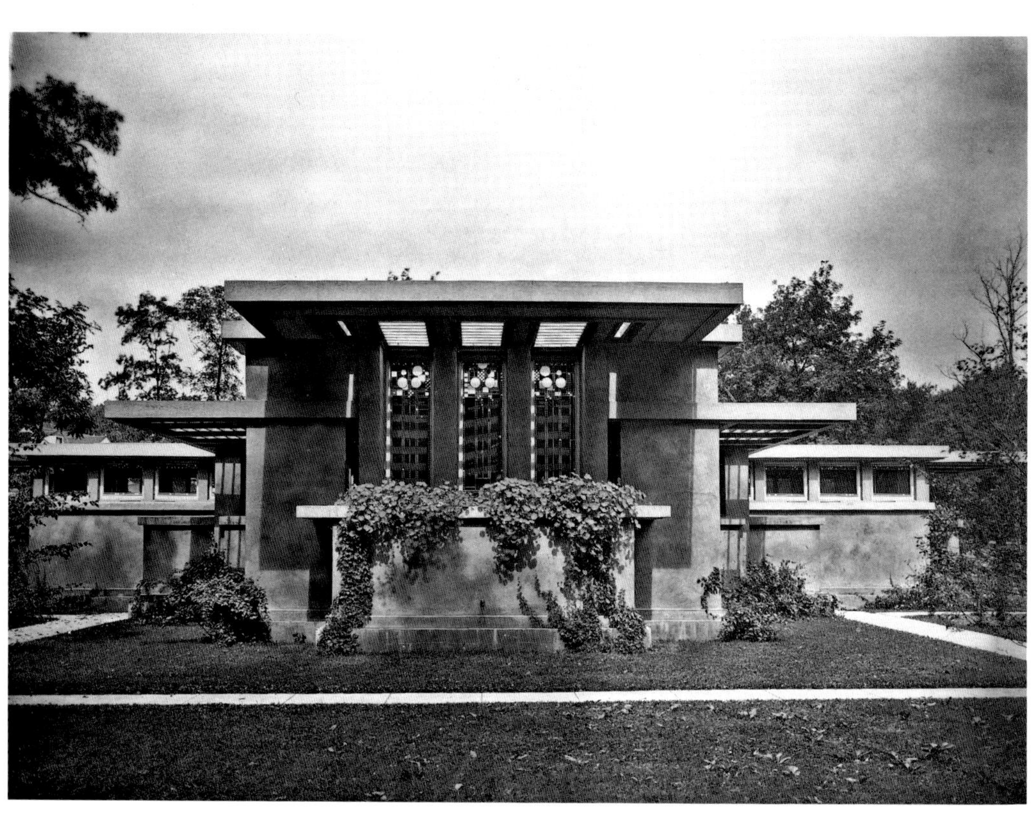

NAME TELEPHONE

ADDRESS

NAME TELEPHONE

ADDRESS

NAME TELEPHONE

ADDRESS

NAME TELEPHONE

ADDRESS

NAME TELEPHONE

ADDRESS

NAME TELEPHONE

ADDRESS

N

NAME TELEPHONE

ADDRESS

NAME TELEPHONE

ADDRESS

NAME TELEPHONE

ADDRESS

NAME TELEPHONE

ADDRESS

NAME TELEPHONE

ADDRESS

NAME TELEPHONE

ADDRESS

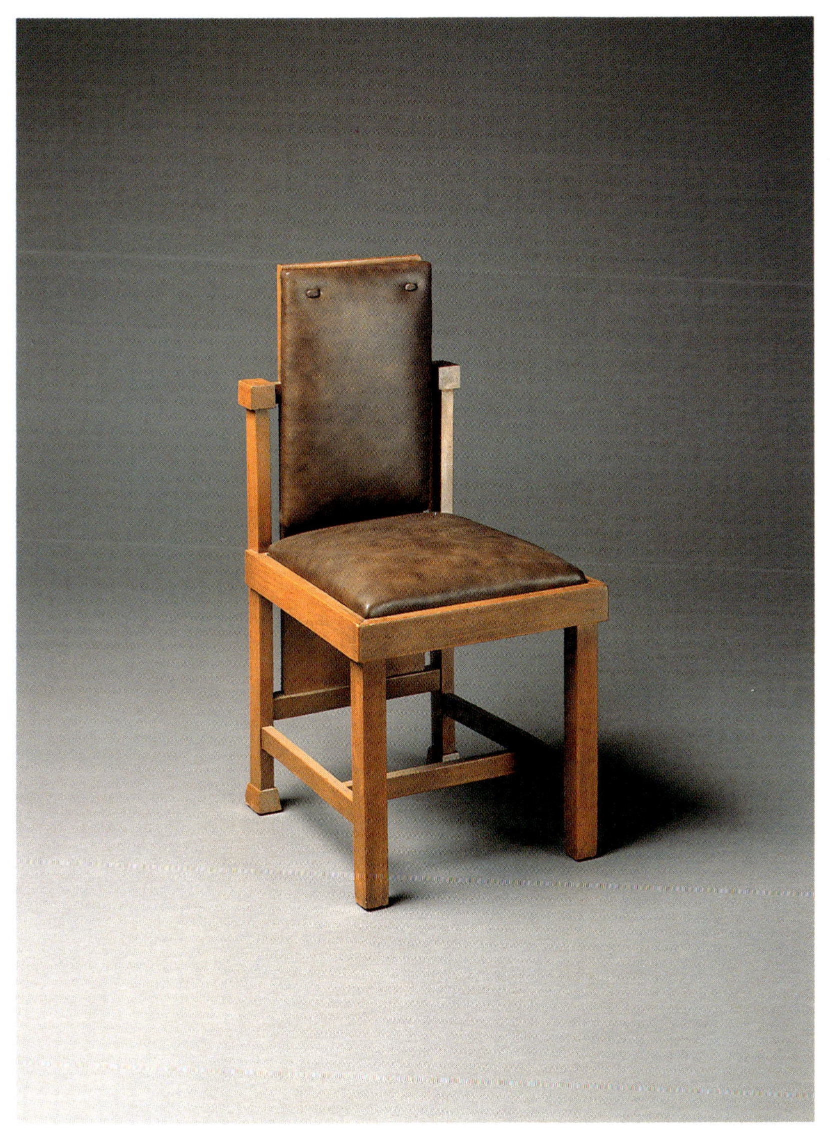

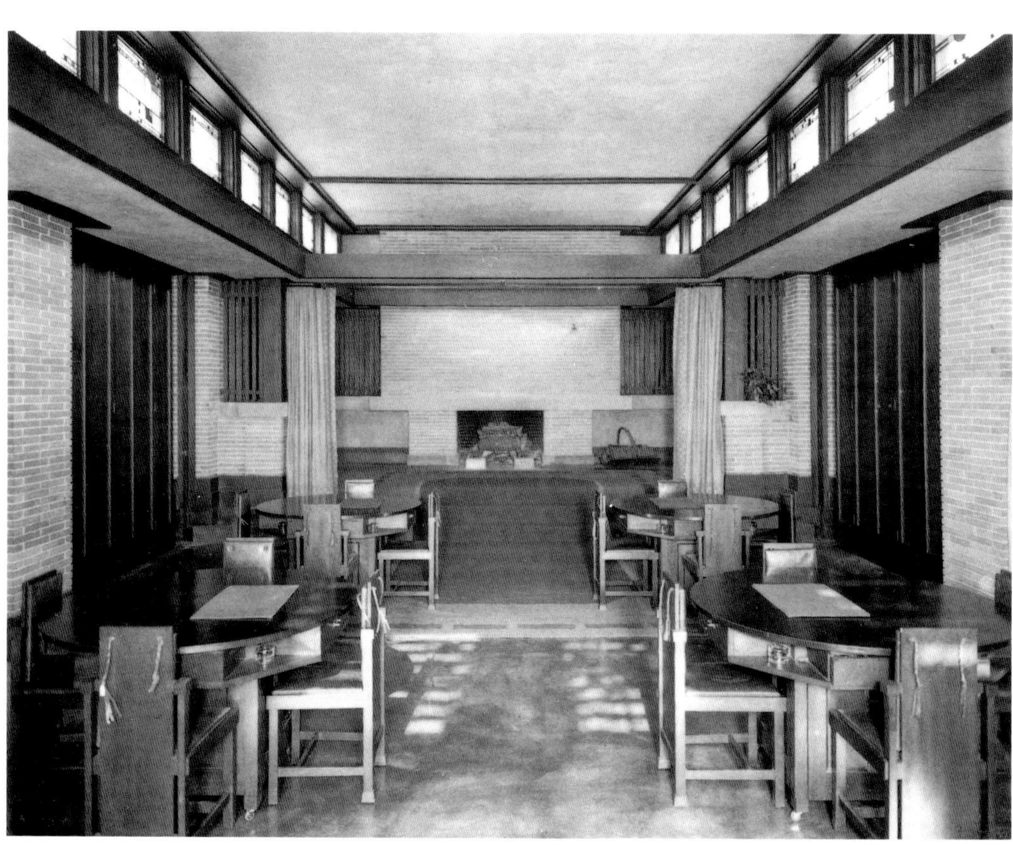

NAME TELEPHONE

ADDRESS

NAME TELEPHONE

ADDRESS

NAME TELEPHONE

ADDRESS

NAME TELEPHONE

ADDRESS

NAME TELEPHONE

ADDRESS

NAME TELEPHONE

ADDRESS

O

NAME TELEPHONE

ADDRESS

NAME TELEPHONE

ADDRESS

NAME TELEPHONE

ADDRESS

NAME TELEPHONE

ADDRESS

NAME TELEPHONE

ADDRESS

NAME TELEPHONE

ADDRESS

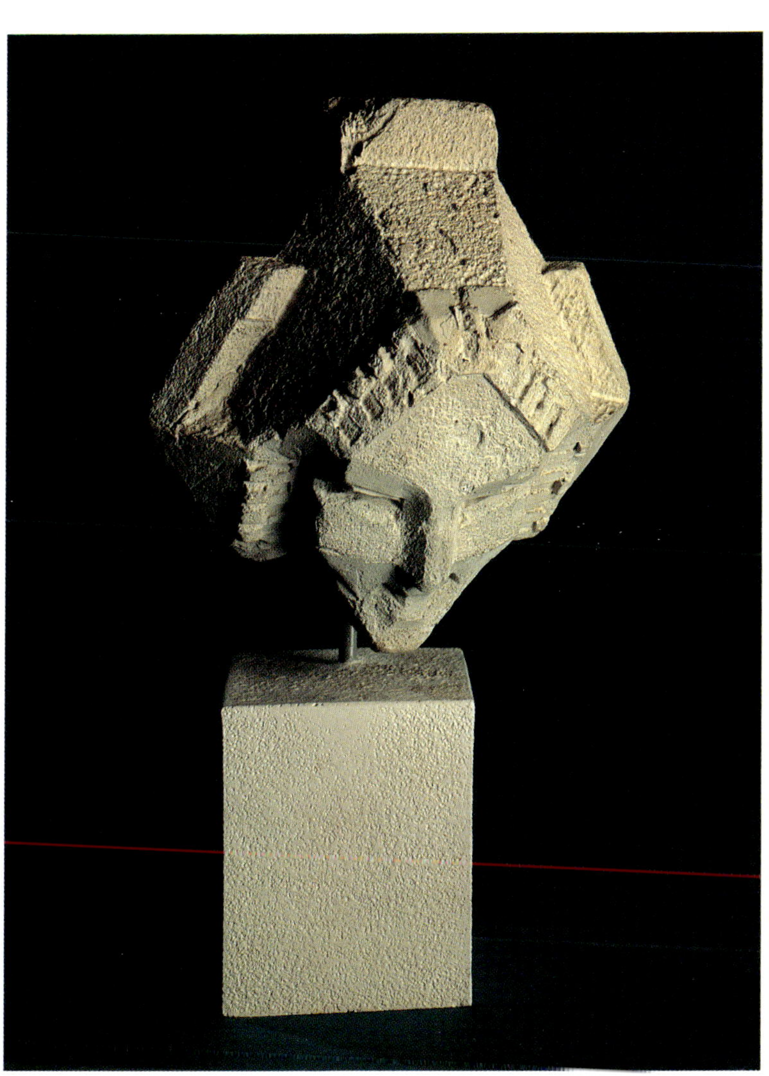

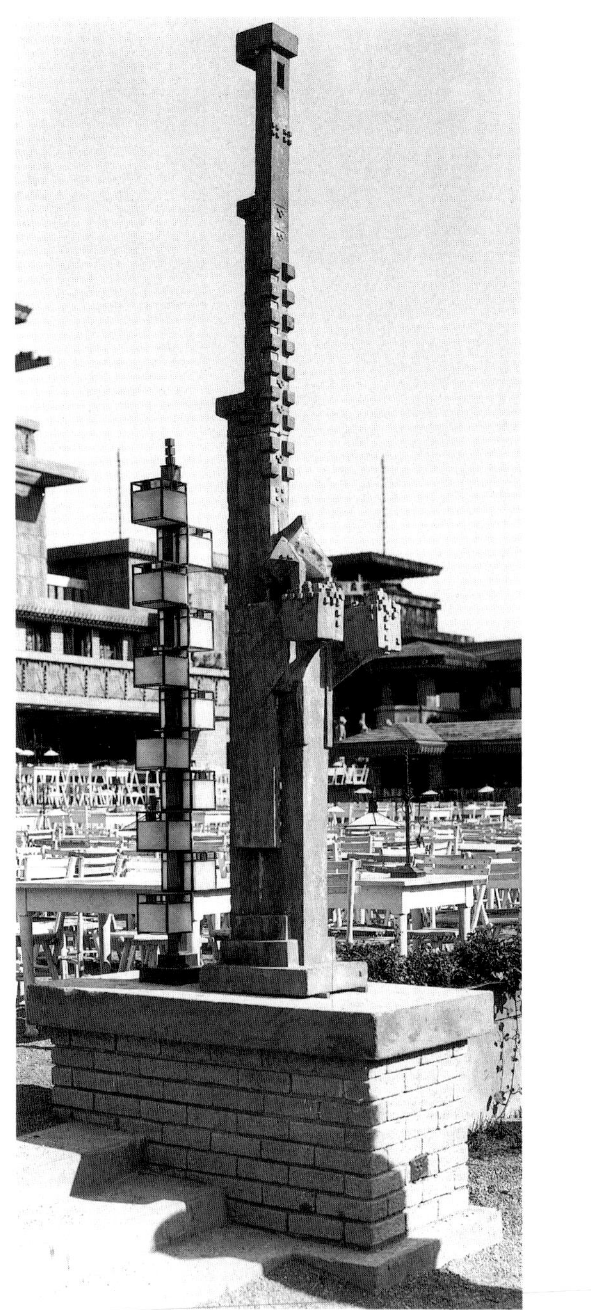

PQ

NAME TELEPHONE

ADDRESS

NAME TELEPHONE

ADDRESS

NAME TELEPHONE

ADDRESS

NAME TELEPHONE

ADDRESS

NAME TELEPHONE

ADDRESS

NAME TELEPHONE

ADDRESS

PQ

NAME TELEPHONE

ADDRESS

NAME TELEPHONE

ADDRESS

NAME TELEPHONE

ADDRESS

NAME TELEPHONE

ADDRESS

NAME TELEPHONE

ADDRESS

NAME TELEPHONE

ADDRESS

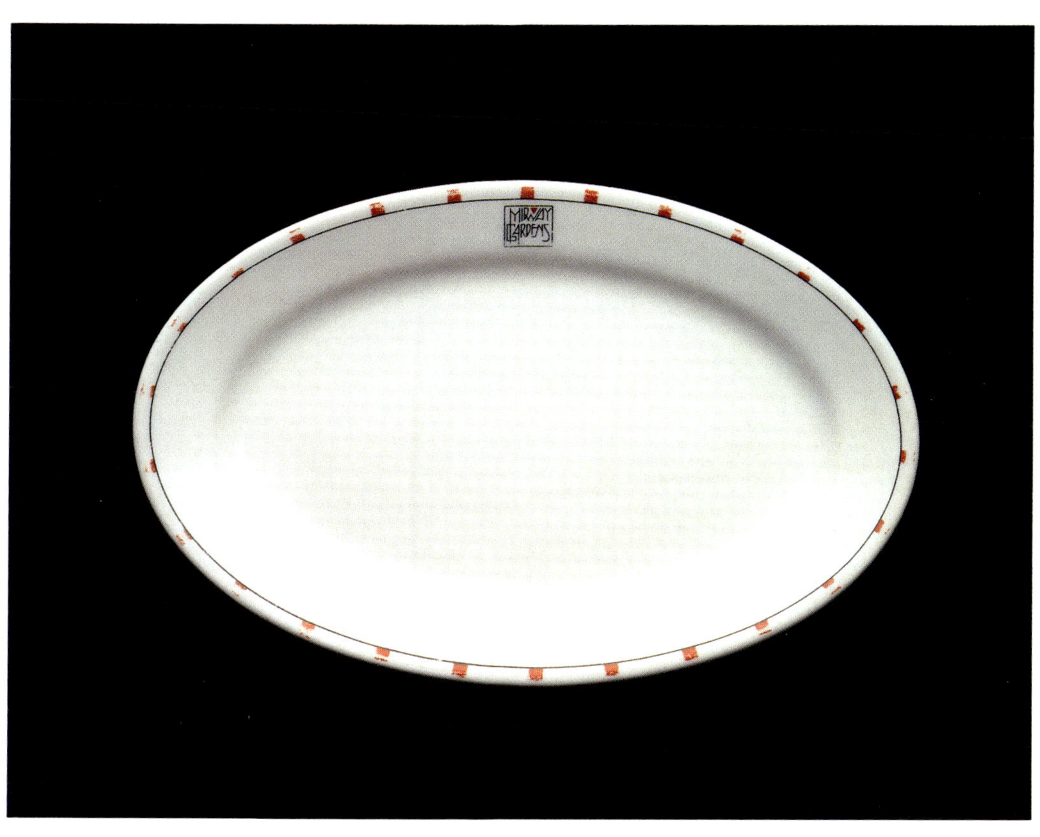

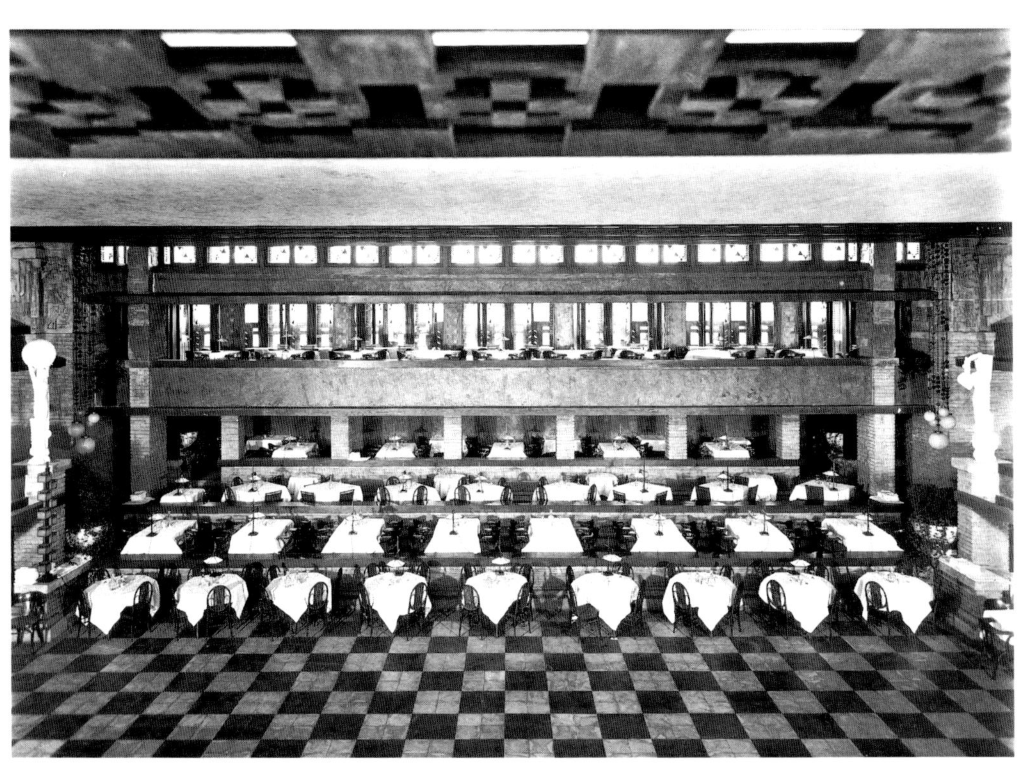

R

NAME TELEPHONE

ADDRESS

NAME TELEPHONE

ADDRESS

NAME TELEPHONE

ADDRESS

NAME TELEPHONE

ADDRESS

NAME TELEPHONE

ADDRESS

NAME TELEPHONE

ADDRESS

R

NAME TELEPHONE

ADDRESS

NAME TELEPHONE

ADDRESS

NAME TELEPHONE

ADDRESS

NAME TELEPHONE

ADDRESS

NAME TELEPHONE

ADDRESS

NAME TELEPHONE

ADDRESS

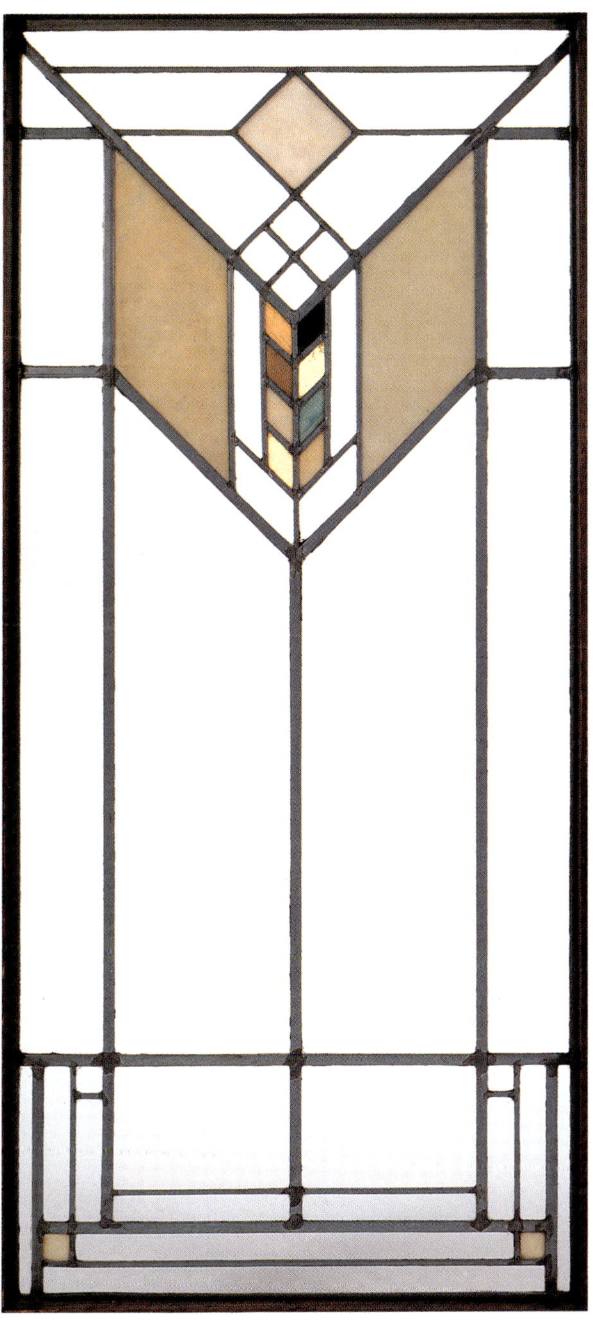

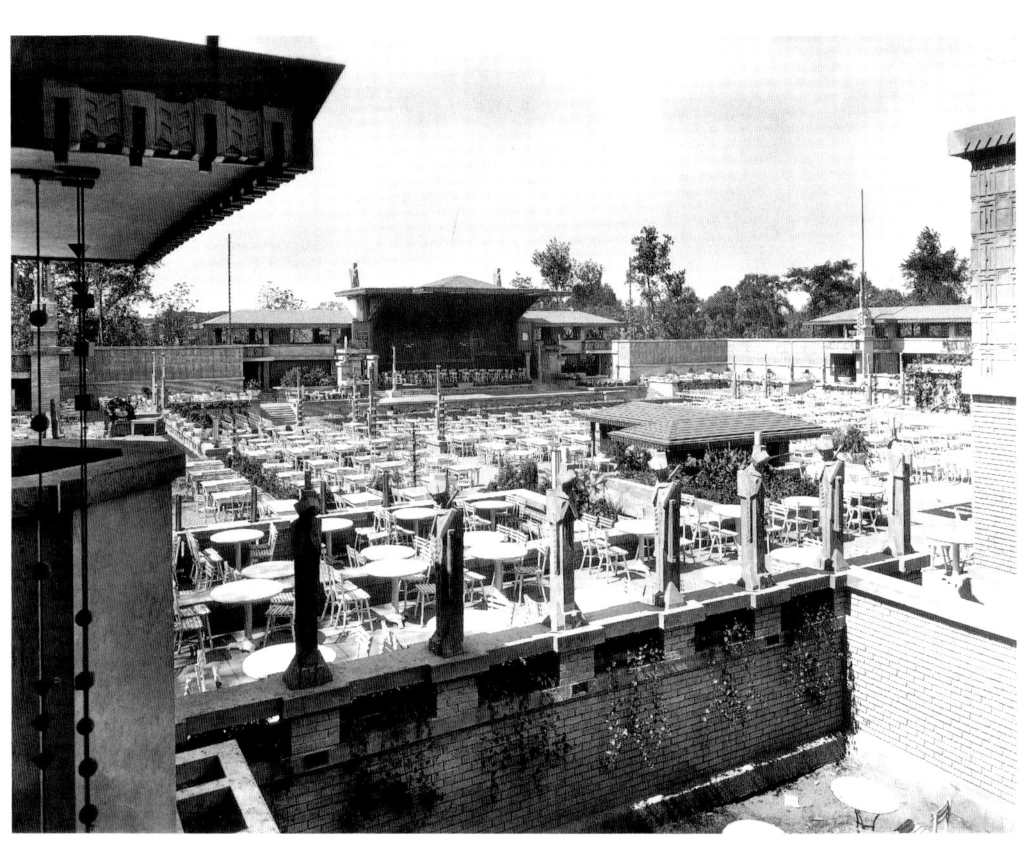

NAME TELEPHONE

ADDRESS

NAME TELEPHONE

ADDRESS

NAME TELEPHONE

ADDRESS

NAME TELEPHONE

ADDRESS

NAME TELEPHONE

ADDRESS

NAME TELEPHONE

ADDRESS

S

NAME TELEPHONE

ADDRESS

NAME TELEPHONE

ADDRESS

NAME TELEPHONE

ADDRESS

NAME TELEPHONE

ADDRESS

NAME TELEPHONE

ADDRESS

NAME TELEPHONE

ADDRESS

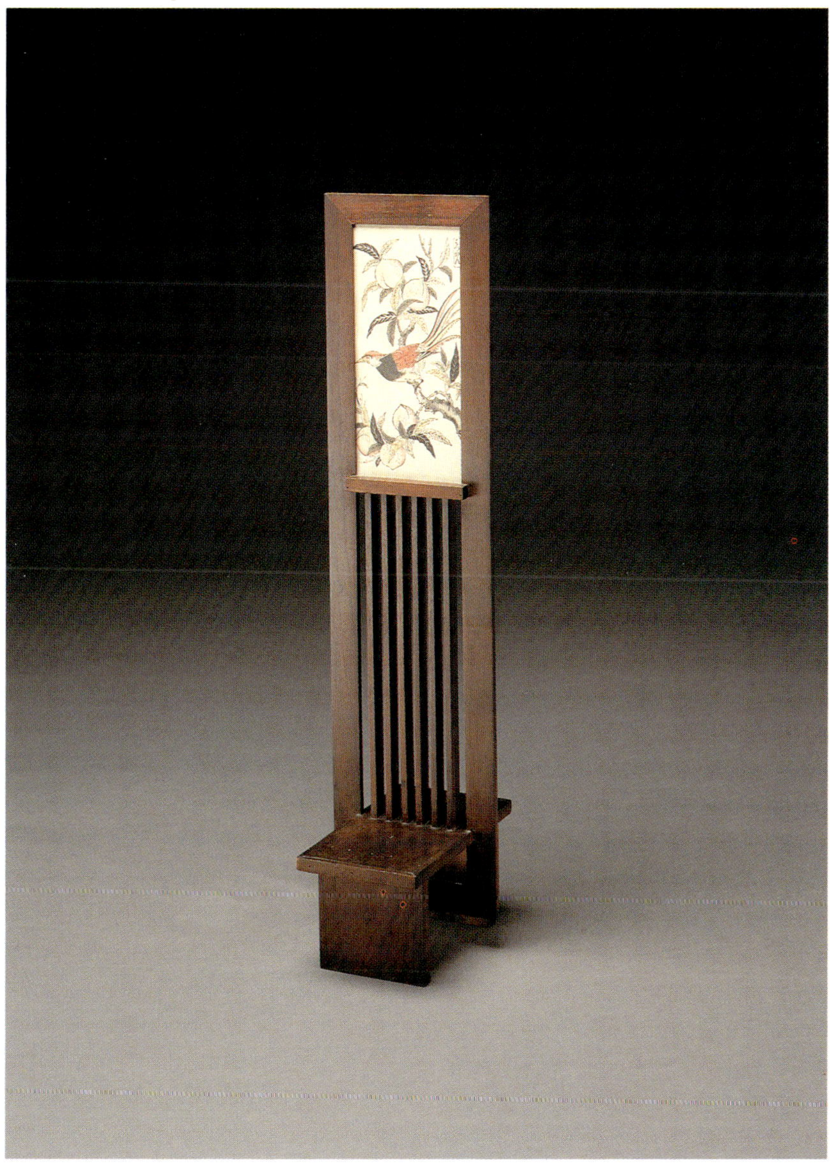

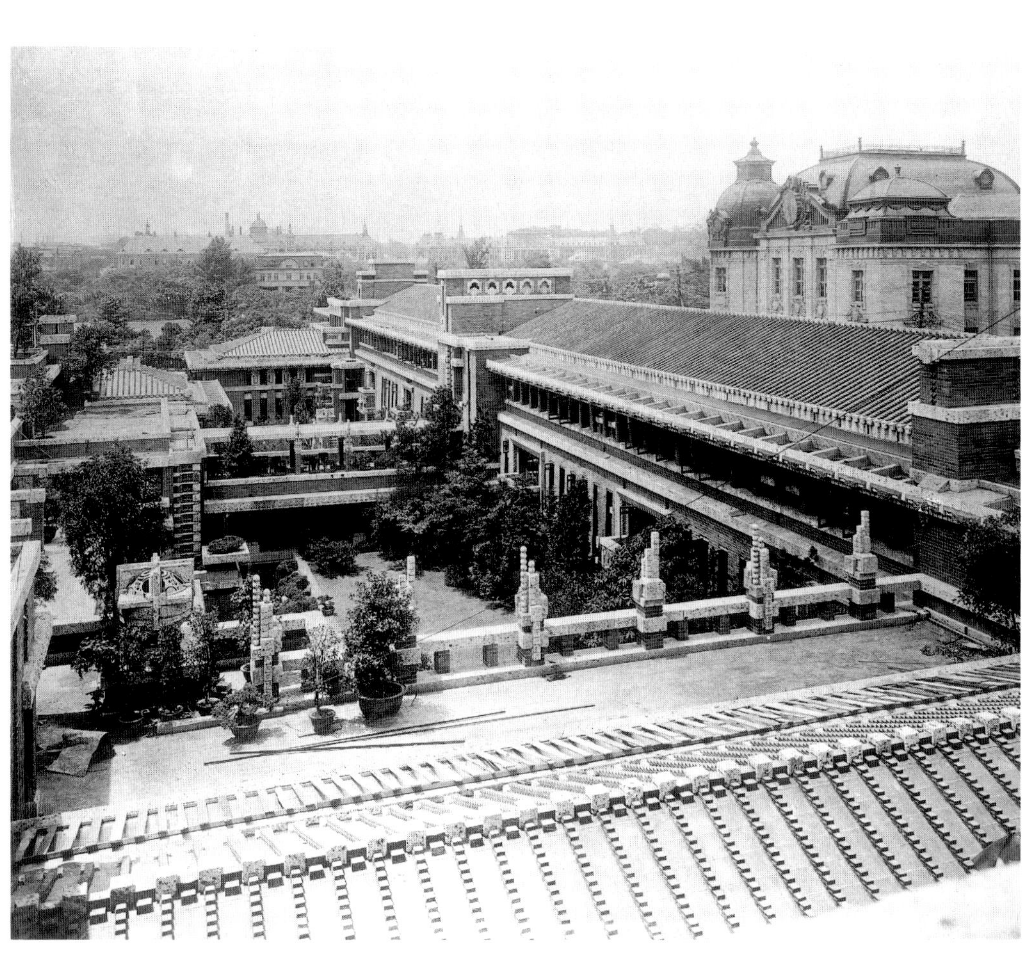

NAME TELEPHONE

ADDRESS

NAME TELEPHONE

ADDRESS

NAME TELEPHONE

ADDRESS

NAME TELEPHONE

ADDRESS

NAME TELEPHONE

ADDRESS

NAME TELEPHONE

ADDRESS

S

NAME TELEPHONE

ADDRESS

NAME TELEPHONE

ADDRESS

NAME TELEPHONE

ADDRESS

NAME TELEPHONE

ADDRESS

NAME TELEPHONE

ADDRESS

NAME TELEPHONE

ADDRESS

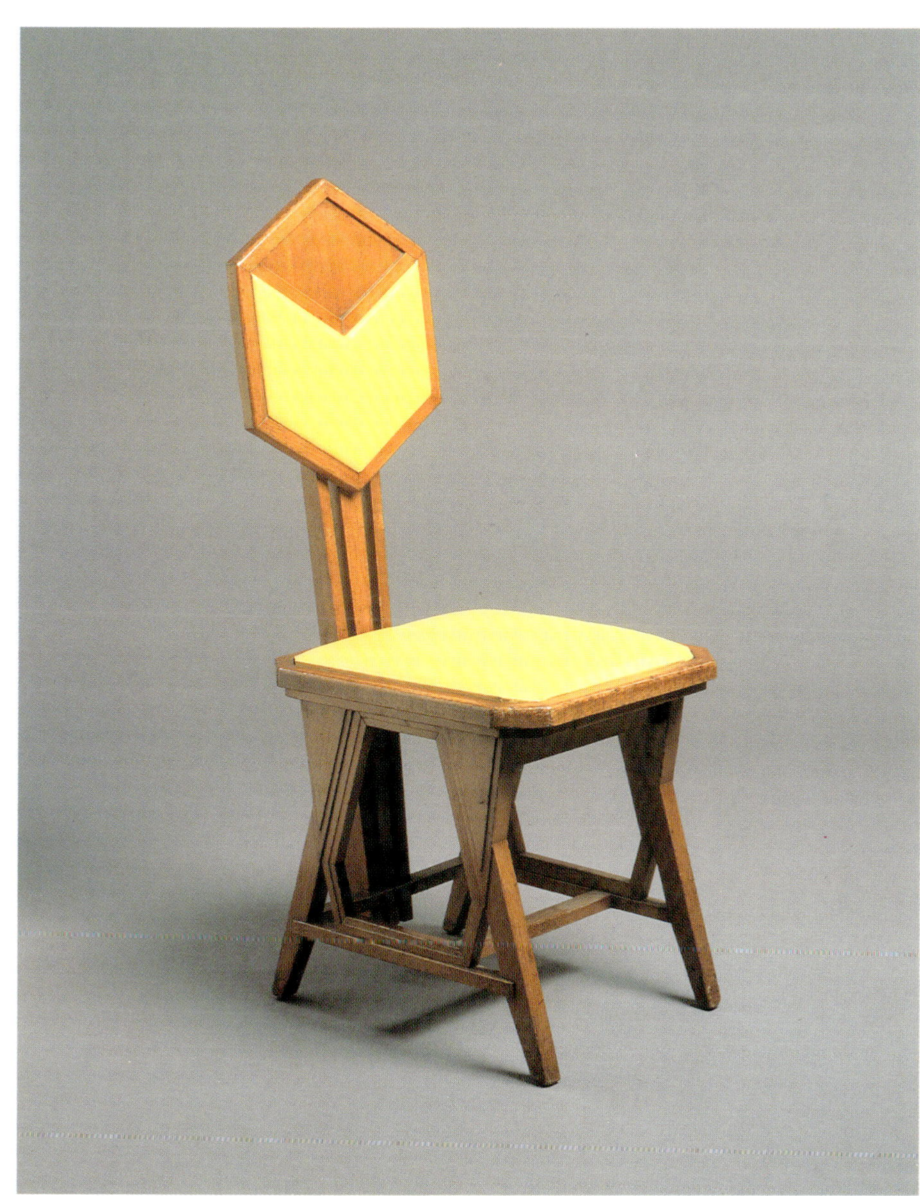

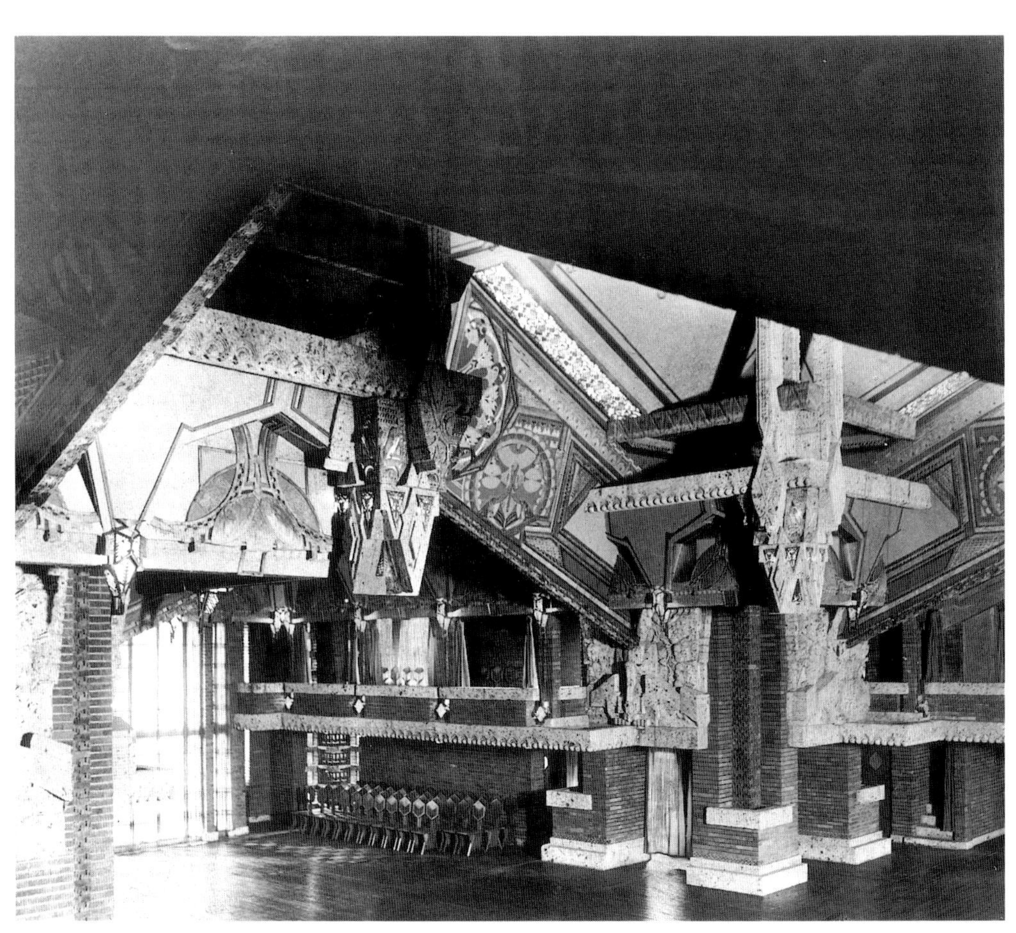

NAME TELEPHONE

ADDRESS

NAME TELEPHONE

ADDRESS

NAME TELEPHONE

ADDRESS

NAME TELEPHONE

ADDRESS

NAME TELEPHONE

ADDRESS

NAME TELEPHONE

ADDRESS

T

NAME TELEPHONE

ADDRESS

NAME TELEPHONE

ADDRESS

NAME TELEPHONE

ADDRESS

NAME TELEPHONE

ADDRESS

NAME TELEPHONE

ADDRESS

NAME TELEPHONE

ADDRESS

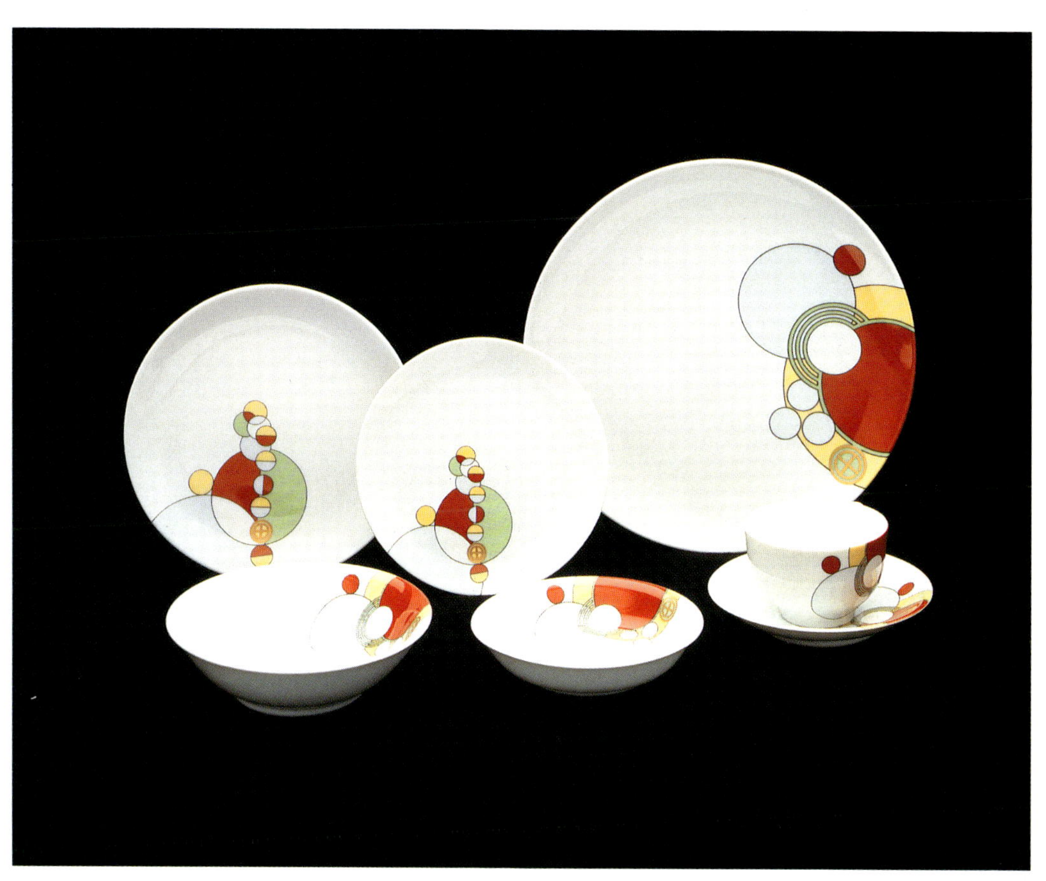

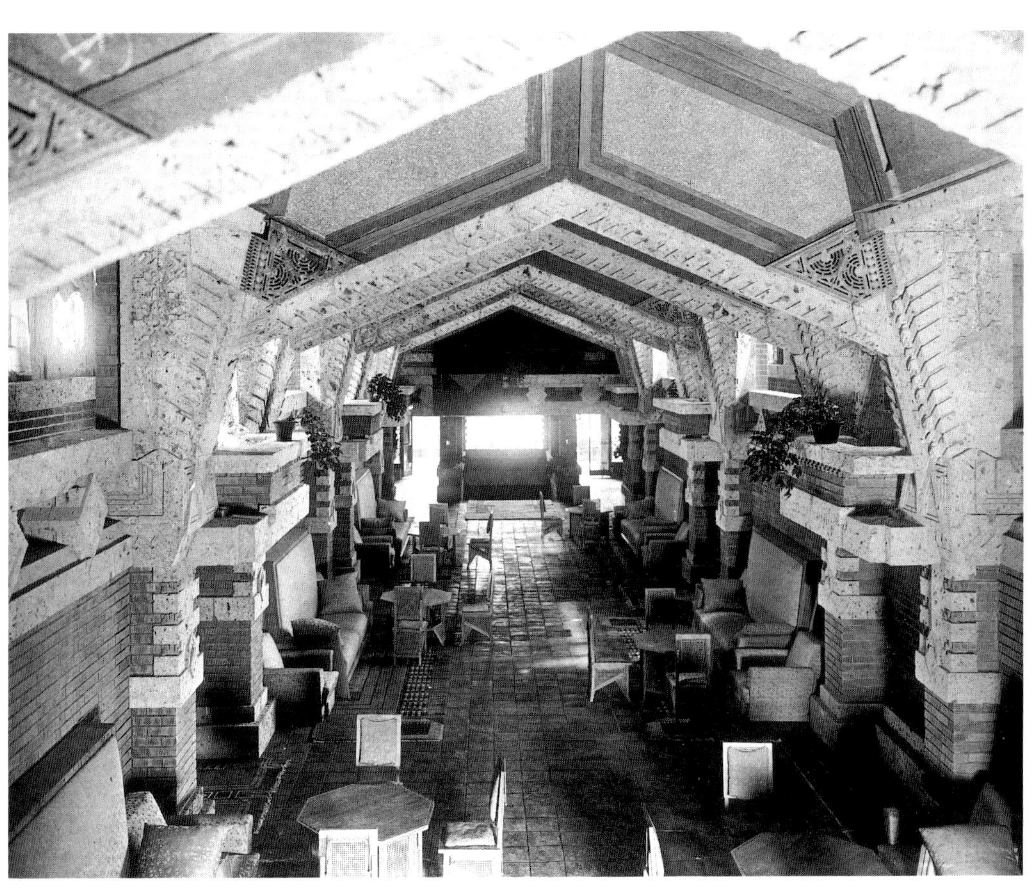

NAME TELEPHONE

ADDRESS

NAME TELEPHONE

ADDRESS

NAME TELEPHONE

ADDRESS

NAME TELEPHONE

ADDRESS

NAME TELEPHONE

ADDRESS

NAME TELEPHONE

ADDRESS

UV

NAME TELEPHONE

ADDRESS

NAME TELEPHONE

ADDRESS

NAME TELEPHONE

ADDRESS

NAME TELEPHONE

ADDRESS

NAME TELEPHONE

ADDRESS

NAME TELEPHONE

ADDRESS

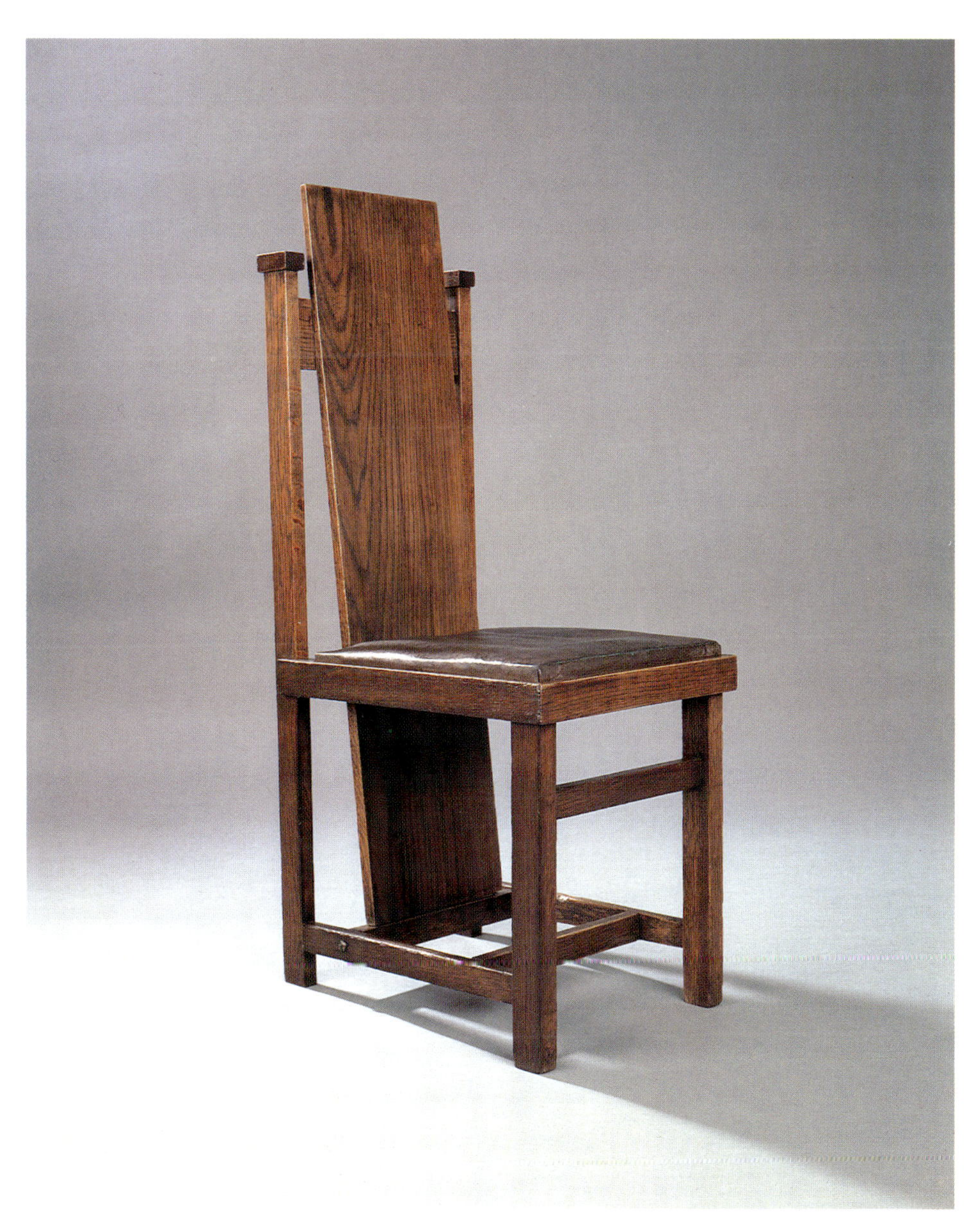

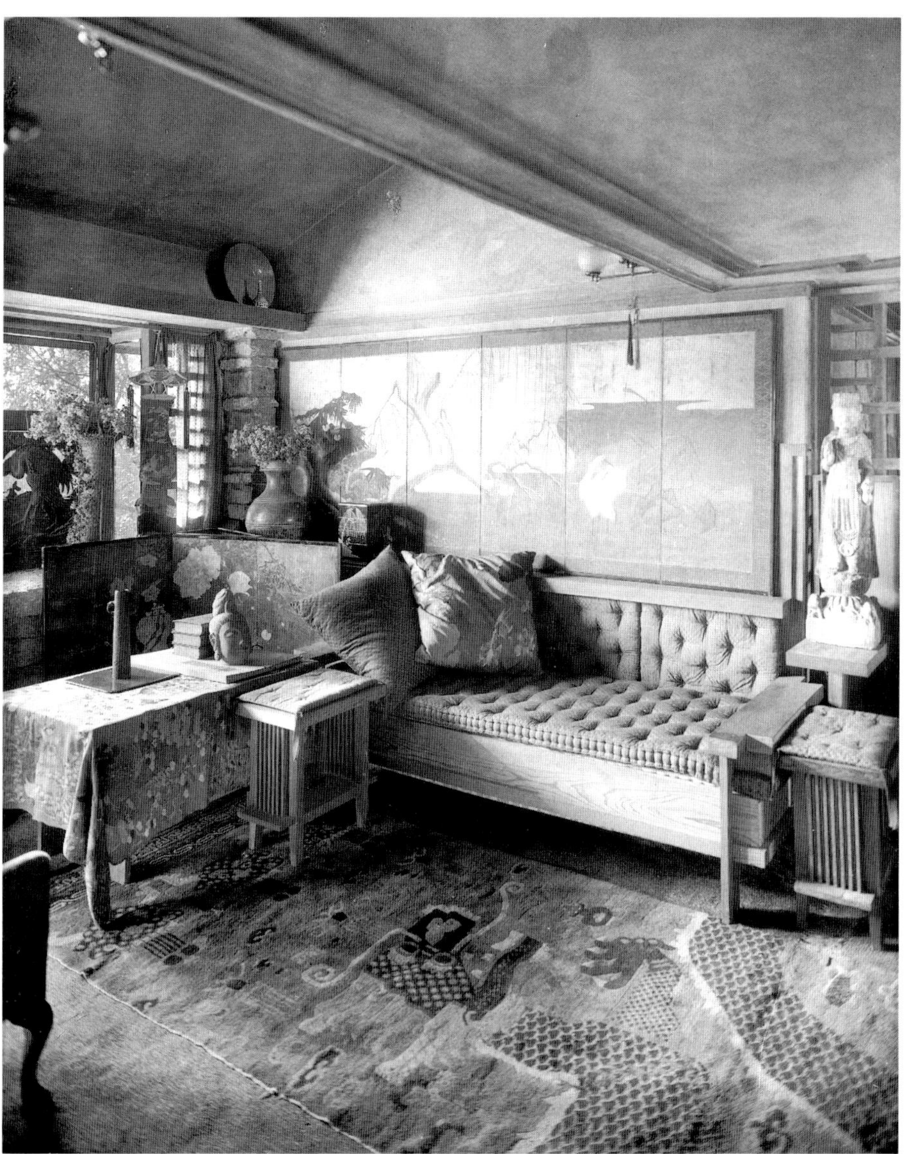

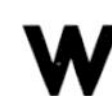

NAME TELEPHONE

ADDRESS

NAME TELEPHONE

ADDRESS

NAME TELEPHONE

ADDRESS

NAME TELEPHONE

ADDRESS

NAME TELEPHONE

ADDRESS

NAME TELEPHONE

ADDRESS

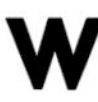

NAME TELEPHONE

ADDRESS

NAME TELEPHONE

ADDRESS

NAME TELEPHONE

ADDRESS

NAME TELEPHONE

ADDRESS

NAME TELEPHONE

ADDRESS

NAME TELEPHONE

ADDRESS

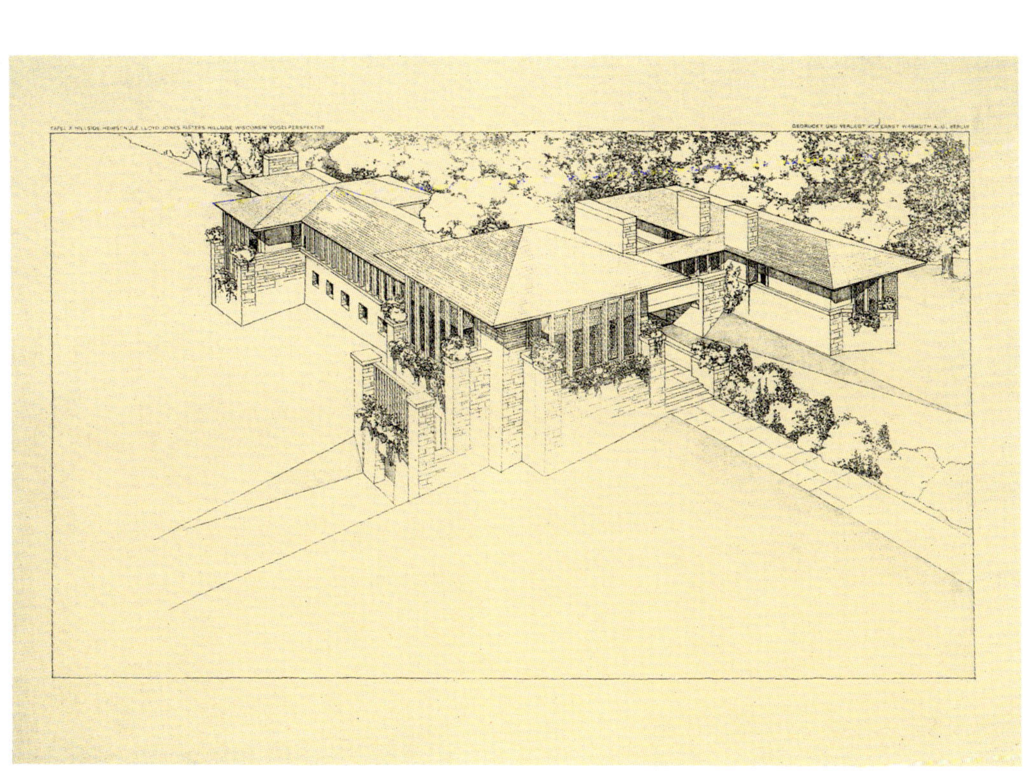
TAFEL X HILLSIDE HEIMSCHULE LLOYD JONES SISTERS HILLSIDE WISCONSIN VOGELPERSPEKTIVE
GEDRUCKT UND VERLEGT VON ERNST WASMUTH A.G. BERLIN

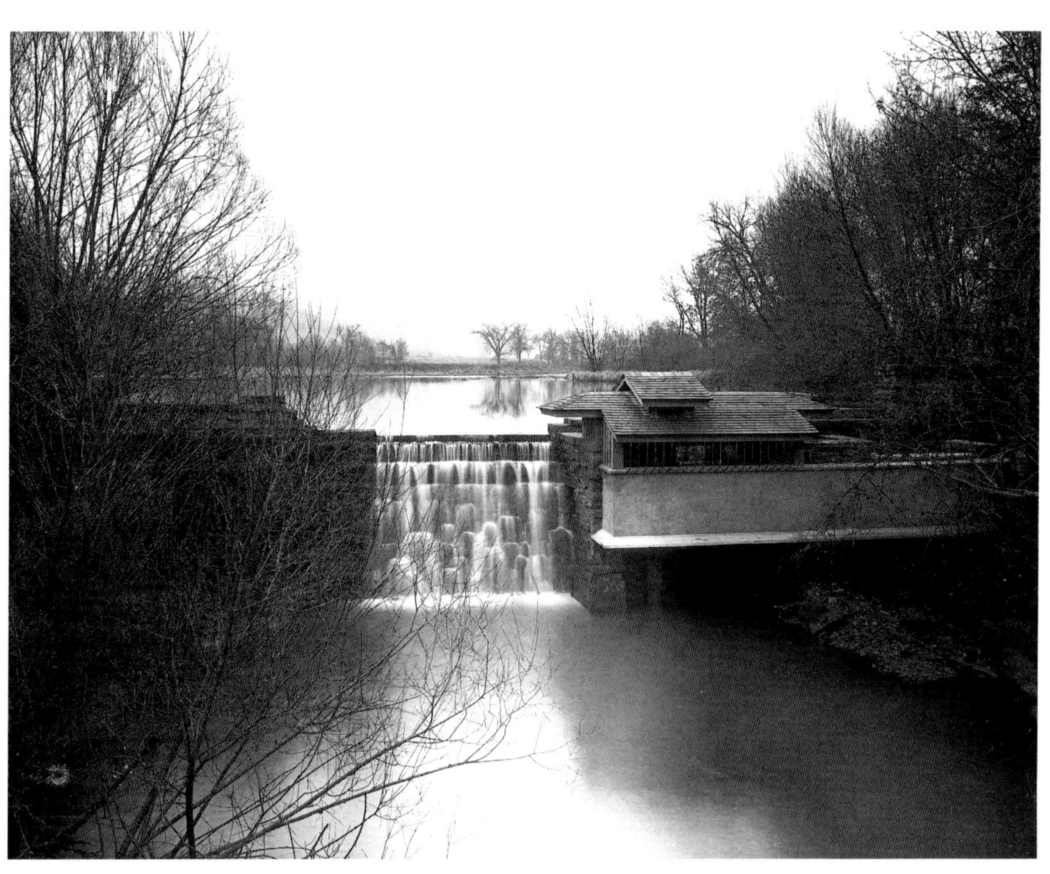

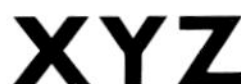

NAME TELEPHONE

ADDRESS

NAME TELEPHONE

ADDRESS

NAME TELEPHONE

ADDRESS

NAME TELEPHONE

ADDRESS

NAME TELEPHONE

ADDRESS

NAME TELEPHONE

ADDRESS

XYZ

NAME TELEPHONE

ADDRESS

NAME TELEPHONE

ADDRESS

NAME TELEPHONE

ADDRESS

NAME TELEPHONE

ADDRESS

NAME TELEPHONE

ADDRESS

NAME TELEPHONE

ADDRESS

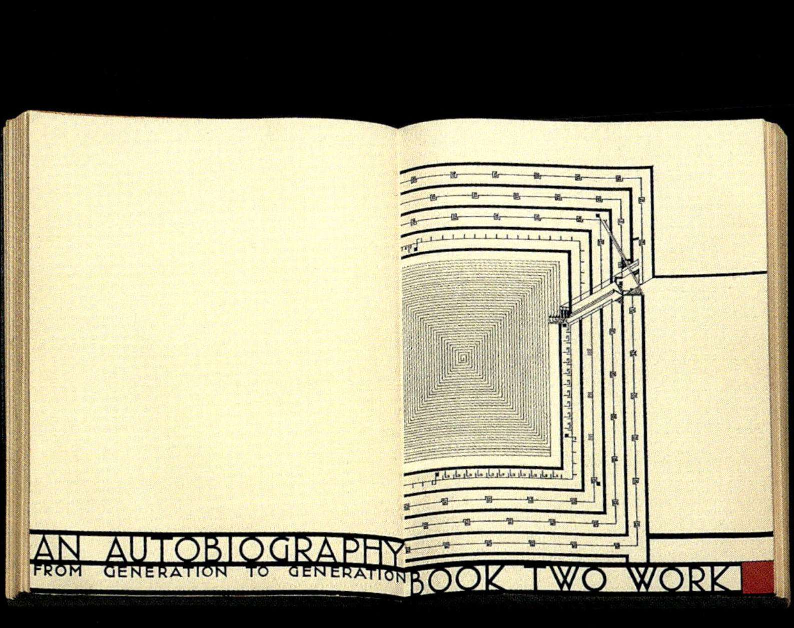
AN AUTOBIOGRAPHY
FROM GENERATION TO GENERATION
BOOK TWO WORK

Illustrations

A: *Sheet copper vase*
Probably from the Wright Home and Studio
Oak Park, Illinois, 1895-1900 (86.26.01)

This vase, or weed holder, was designed in the late 1890s at the start of Wright's independent practice. Wright featured this design in several early interiors, including the octagonal library in his Oak Park studio.

Exterior of the Frank Lloyd Wright Home and Studio
Oak Park, Illinois, 1889-1895 (85)

In his home and studio, Wright experimented with new ideas for architecture and design.

Pair of gates
Nathan G. Moore house
Oak Park, Illinois, c.1895 (88.05.01a&b)

These gates represented a compromise between the client's interest in gothic architecture and Wright's geometric style.

Exterior of the Nathan G. Moore house
Oak Park, Illinois, 1895 (54)

In this early commission, the client requested that Wright design a house in the English Tudor style.

B: *Copper urn*
Wright Home and Studio
Oak Park, Illinois, 1895 (85.04.01)

This urn was one of Wright's favorite objects and appeared in a number of interiors, including the Edward C. Waller house, River Forest, Illinois, and the Susan Lawrence Dana house, Springfield, Illinois.

Interior of the Edward C. Waller house
River Forest, Illinois, 1899 (75)

In Wright's remodeling of this home, the circular shapes of the stair balusters were echoed in the decorative urn.

C: *Clerestory window*
Warren Hickox house
Kankakee, Illinois, 1900 (87.06.01)

Wright's leaded-glass window design reflected angles in the roof.

Exterior of the Warren Hickox house
Kankakee, Illinois, 1900 (49)

Arthur Heurtley house, Oak Park, Illinois, 1902;
Wasmuth rendering and floor plan
Plate XX *Ausgeführte Bauten und Entwürfe von Frank Lloyd Wright* (Studies and Executed Buildings by Frank Lloyd Wright). First edition printed 1910 (86.08.07)

In 1909, Wright was approached by the German publisher, Ernst Wasmuth, to publish a two-volume portfolio of his architectural drawings. The completed Wasmuth portfolio was a publisher's masterpiece and contributed to Wright's international renown.

Exterior of the Arthur Heurtley house
Oak Park, Illinois, 1902 (47)

In this early example of Prairie architecture, Wright created horizontal bands by staggering the Roman brick.

D: *Reclining armchair*
Arthur Heurtley house
Oak Park, Illinois, 1902 (86.01.01)

The design of this birch, elm, and leather chair was in harmony with the angled configurations of the architecture.

Living room of the Arthur Heurtley house
Oak Park, Illinois, 1902 (48)

EF: *Dining chair*
Ward W. Willits house
Highland Park, Illinois, 1902 (86.34.10)

Tall, oak chairs were a major element of Wright's early dining rooms. Their backs featured slender vertical slats as an integral ornament. By creating a "screen" effect when grouped around a table, such chairs defined an intimate "room within a room."

Exterior of the Ward W. Willits house
Highland Park, Illinois, 1902 (76)

Pair of casement windows and transom
B. Harley Bradley house
Kankakee, Illinois, c.1900 (86.06.01a-c)

These leaded-glass windows were among Wright's earliest designs incorporating stylized floral motifs.

Interior of Unity Temple
Oak Park, Illinois, 1904 (138)

Wright's innovative design for Unity Temple featured poured concrete construction.

G: *Windows*
Avery Coonley house
Riverside, Illinois, 1908 (86.20.4a and 86.20.4b)

In this leaded-glass design, Wright mirrored the effect of ivy in planter boxes on the exterior of the house.

Exterior of the Avery Coonley house
Riverside, Illinois, 1908 (8)

This photograph captured the harmonious relationship of the Coonley gardens and residence as they originally existed. The Coonley family is pictured in this view.

H: *Library table*
Avery Coonley house
Riverside, Illinois, 1908 (87.17.18)

As in many Wright homes, most of the original furniture was subsequently removed. This library table can be seen in the photograph of the Coonley living room (next page).

Living room of the Avery Coonley house
Riverside, Illinois, 1908 (19)

"Mrs. Coonley said they had come because it seemed to them they saw in my houses 'the countenance of principle.' This was to me a great and sincere compliment. Looking back upon it, I feel now that that building was the best I could then do in the way of a house." (Frank Lloyd Wright, *An Autobiography,* 1932)

IJ: *Wall sconce*
Avery Coonley house
Riverside, Illinois, 1908 (86.20.06)

Light played an important role in Wright's architectural environments. This sconce repeated a fern motif used throughout the room.

Living room and hallway of the Avery Coonley house
Riverside, Illinois, 1908 (25)

The mural of birch trees and ferns was designed and painted by George Niedecken.

K: *Armchair*
Ray W. Evans house
Chicago, Illinois, c.1908 (86.08.05)

The original finish, which corresponded to the interior woodwork in the house, was subsequently painted over. The armchair has now been restored to its original color.

Dining room of the Ray W. Evans house
Chicago, Illinois, 1908 (42)

Tables with massive tops and slatted bases were characteristic of Wright's Prairie dining rooms.

L: *Oak chair*
Isabel Roberts house
River Forest, Illinois, c.1908 (86.01.06)

This oak and leather chair was similar to one that Wright designed for the dining room of his Oak Park home.

Interior of the Isabel Roberts house
River Forest, Illinois, 1908 (60)

Wall sconce
Peter A. Beachy house
Oak Park, Illinois, 1906 (86.05.03)

The configuration of the sconce mirrored angles in the gabled roof.

Exterior of the Frederick C. Robie house
Chicago, Illinois, 1908 (64)

The Robie house was one of Wright's Prairie masterpieces. Its triangular bays have been likened to the prow of a ship.

M: *Dining room sideboard*
William B. Greene house
Aurora, Illinois, 1912 (86.08.06)

Wright often designed built-in furniture as an integral part of his interiors.

Dining room and hallway of the Frederick C. Robie house
Chicago, Illinois, 1909 (70)

The dining table, with lamps positioned at each corner, was not unique to the Robie house. Wright designed similar dining tables for other Prairie houses, including the Darwin D. Martin house, Buffalo, New York, and the Meyer May house, Grand Rapids, Michigan.

N: *Clerestory window*
Avery Coonley Playhouse
Riverside, Illinois, c.1912 (86.06.05)

Wright's leaded-glass designs for the Coonley Playhouse were inspired by balloons, confetti, and flags in a parade. They represent Wright's earliest use of primary colors, influenced by the art of the European avante-garde.

Exterior of the Avery Coonley Playhouse
Riverside, Illinois, 1912 (29)

Returning from a pivotal trip to Europe, Wright received a second commission from the Coonley family to design a small building for a progressive school.

Child's side chair
Avery Coonley Playhouse
Riverside, Illinois, 1912 (85.02.04)

This birch and leather chair incorporated simple forms and minimal ornament to facilitate production by craftsmen using machines.

Avery Coonley Playhouse theater
Riverside, Illinois, 1912 (30)

Wright's design contained a stage for children's theatrical productions.

O: *Sprite head sculpture*
Midway Gardens
Chicago, Illinois, c.1914 (87.05.01)

Midway Gardens was an entertainment complex that enclosed an entire city block. Here, Wright attempted to unite architecture with sculpture and painting. The extensive sculpture, executed by Wright's assistants, Alfonso Iannelli and Richard Bock, recalled the work of the Cubists.

Sculpture in the Summer Garden at Midway Gardens
Chicago, Illinois, 1914 (143)

PQ: *Plate*
Midway Gardens
Chicago, Illinois, c.1914 (86.03.04)

"It swarmed with exquisitely gowned women and men in evening attire—a brilliant social affair. . . . I could see Pavlova dancing in the open air pavilion surrounded by balconies, terraces, (and) urns overflowing with flowers." (John L. Wright, *My Father Who is on Earth,* 1946)

Interior dining area at Midway Gardens
Chicago, Illinois, 1914 (158)

Prohibition in 1920 brought on the decline of the Midway Gardens. It was demolished in 1929.

R: *Window*
Geneva Inn
Lake Geneva, Wisconsin, 1911 (85.01.02)

In response to the mobility afforded by the automobile, developer Arthur Richards commissioned Wright to design an elegant resort overlooking Lake Geneva, Wisconsin. The hotel was neither built exactly as Wright designed it nor with his supervision, but the 360-foot-long Prairie style building retained many of the architect's unique features.

View of the Summer Gardens at Midway Gardens
Chicago, Illinois, 1914 (168)

"The Midway Gardens were planned as a summer garden: a system of low masonry terraces enclosed by promenades, loggias and galleries at the sides, these flanked by the Winter Garden. The Winter Garden also was terraced and balconied in permanent masonry without and within. This Winter Garden stood on the main street, opposite the great orchestra shell." (Frank Lloyd Wright, *An Autobiography*, 1932)

S: *Mahogany Print Stand,* Japanese print (not original to stand) c.1908 (86.08.13)

"If Japanese prints were to be deducted from my education, I don't know what direction the whole might have taken." (Frank Lloyd Wright, *An Autobiography,* 1932)

Exterior of the Imperial Hotel
Tokyo, Japan, 1916-1922 (186)

Brick and oya stone—a soft, textural lava—contributed to the exotic character of Wright's only non-American architectural commission.

Chair
Imperial Hotel
Tokyo, Japan, 1916-1922;
this example from c.1930 (86.01.03)

Wright's repetition of the hexagon was visible in the hotel's ceiling, tables, and oak chairs with oil-cloth upholstery.

Interior of the Imperial Hotel
Tokyo, Japan, 1916-1922 (175)

When the hotel was razed in 1968, the lobby entrance was dismantled and preserved. It was reconstructed in 1976 at the Meiji Village, an open-air museum 230 miles west of Tokyo.

T: *Place setting*
Imperial Hotel
Tokyo, Japan, 1916-1922;
this example from 1964-1966 (87.16.01-06)

The design of the porcelain for the Imperial Hotel was reminiscent of the Coonley Playhouse windows and painted murals at Midway Gardens.

Interior of the Imperial Hotel
Tokyo, Japan, 1916-1922 (176)

UV: *Chair*
Hillside Home School
Spring Green, Wisconsin, c.1904 (86.34.05)

As with other Wright furnishings, this chair featured simple, geometric forms, devoid of applied ornament.

Interior of Taliesin East
Spring Green, Wisconsin, 1911- (116)

Taliesin's rustic ambiance provided an intriguing backdrop for Wright's changing arrangements of oriental carpets and art.

W: *Hillside Home School*
Spring Green, Wisconsin, 1902;
Wasmuth rendering of exterior
Plate X *Ausgeführte Bauten und Entwürfe von Frank Lloyd Wright* (Studies and Executed Buildings by Frank Lloyd Wright). First edition printed 1910 (86.08.07)

The original Hillside Home School, a Wright design of 1887, was demolished in 1956. A second school was built for Wright's aunts circa 1903. In the 1920s the school was closed and the building stood empty until the 1930s. When the Taliesin Fellowship was formed, Wright added a drafting room, dining room, and theater. Today, the school is an important part of the Taliesin East complex.

Taliesin East exterior
Spring Green, Wisconsin, 1911- (126)

"A building should appear to grow easily from its site and be shaped to harmonize with its surroundings if Nature is manifest there; and if not try to make it as quiet, substantial and organic as She would have been were the opportunity Hers." ("In the Cause of Architecture," *Architectural Record*, 1908)

XYZ: *An Autobiography*
Published by Longmans, Green, and Company, 1932 (86.23.100)

Wright's *An Autobiography* was praised in a contemporary review as a book "that compares in brilliance and originality with his buildings . . ."